Harvard Business Review

ON

NONPROFITS

D0030708

THE HARVARD BUSINESS REVIEW PAPERBACK SERIES

The series is designed to bring today's managers and professionals the fundamental information they need to stay competitive in a fast-moving world. From the preeminent thinkers whose work has defined an entire field to the rising stars who will redefine the way we think about business, here are the leading minds and landmark ideas that have established the *Harvard Business Review* as required reading for ambitious businesspeople in organizations around the globe.

Harvard Business Review

ON

NONPROFITS

A HARVARD BUSINESS REVIEW PAPERBACK

The *Harvard Business Review* articles in this collection are available as individual reprints. Discounts apply to quantity purchases. For information and ordering, please contact Customer Service, Harvard Business School Publishing, Boston, MA 02163. Telephone: (617) 783-7500 or (800) 988-0886, 8 A.M. to 6 P.M. Eastern Time, Monday through Friday. Fax: (617) 783-7555, 24 hours a day. E-mail: custserv@hbsp.harvard.edu

Library of Congress Cataloging-in-Publication Data
Harvard business review on nonprofits.
    p. cm.— (A Harvard business review paperback)
    Includes index.
    ISBN 0-87584-909-1 (alk. paper)
    1. Nonprofit organizations—Management. 2. Nonprofit organizations—Finance. I. Harvard business review. II. Series: Harvard business review paperback series.
HD62.6.H366 1999
658'.048—dc21

                               98-31398
                                 CIP

The paper used in this publication meets the requirements of the American National Standard for Permanence of Paper for Printed Library Materials Z39.49-1984.

Contents

Harvard Business Review

ON

NONPROFITS

Can Public Trust in Nonprofits and Governments Be Restored?

REGINA E. HERZLINGER

Executive Summary

WE ENTRUST NONPROFIT AND GOVERNMENTAL ORGANIZATIONS with society's most important functions—educating our minds, uplifting our souls, and protecting our health and safety. Lately, however, the public's faith in these institutions has been seriously undermined by revelations of wrongdoing and mismanagement. Can anything be done to restore the public's confidence?

Regina Herzlinger argues forcefully that the answer lies in accountability. She points out that nonprofits and governments lack the mechanisms that compel accountability in the business world. Thus they require regulatory oversight to help them accomplish their social missions effectively, efficiently, and responsibly.

Drawing on the SEC's history of successfully regulating securities trading, Herzlinger outlines a remedy she calls DADS. Her plan would require nonprofits and governments to increase the *disclosure, analysis,* and *dissemination* of performance information and would apply *sanctions* against organizations that do not comply with those requirements. In particular, the author stresses the need for the disclosure of nonfinancial quantitative information as a way to determine if organizations such as schools and hospitals are fulfilling their missions. And she provides an example of how analysis might work in practice by applying her ideas retrospectively to the bankruptcy of Orange County, California, and by showing how it might have been avoided.

Finally, she calls on managers and overseers of nonprofits and governments, members of the public, and elected officials to undertake the difficult work of restoring public trust in these important institutions.

WHEN GOVERNMENTAL AND NONPROFIT ORGANIZATIONS ARE GOOD, they are very good. And good they must be, because we entrust them with society's most important functions—educating our minds, uplifting our souls, and protecting our health and safety. Our collective perception of their value is evident in the monumental resources we devote to these institutions: Revenues of nonprofits alone have grown from less than $200 billion in 1978 to $1.1 trillion in 1993.

But when governmental and nonprofit organizations are bad, they are horrid. The former president of the United Way of America, possibly the country's premier nonprofit organization, was sentenced to prison in 1995 for defrauding the organization of $1.2 million. Revelations about his $463,000 compensation package and lavish spending caused a drastic drop-off in revenue and a layoff of more than 100 employees. And the distinguished 86-year-old National Association for the Advancement of Colored People sustained a similarly heavy blow when the public learned in 1994 that its executive director had been dismissed for giving $332,000 of the association's funds to a former employee who had alleged sexual harassment.

The performance of nonprofits and governments is shrouded behind a veil of secrecy that is lifted only when disasters occur.

Governmental organizations are not immune from severe problems either. In 1995, the former treasurer of California's Orange County, widely held to be responsible for the largest municipal bankruptcy the United States has ever known, pleaded guilty to six felonies. The county was forced to lay off more than 1,000 employees.

Are such problems idiosyncratic or systemic? Do they reflect a few bad apples or do they characterize the entire nonprofit and government sectors? The plain fact is that we cannot answer these questions. Unlike publicly traded corporations, the performance of nonprofits and governments is shrouded behind a veil of secrecy that is lifted only when blatant disasters occur. At the same time, these questions have gained urgency because of the growing disenchantment of the U.S. public with the federal government—a mood that has led to calls for greater reliance on nonprofit organizations and local governments to solve important social problems. Unless we are provided with credible, systematic information, fresh

scandals will fill our daily newspapers and public trust in
these critically important institutions will erode.

Four Problems—and No Accountability

The difficulties manifested in nonprofit and governmental organizations fall into four categories. First is the
problem of *ineffective* organizations; that is, ones that do
not accomplish their social missions. Consider two
examples: Chicago's Postal Service, whose employees
discarded vast amounts of mail, and nonprofit hospitals
that "dump" medically unstable patients who cannot
afford to pay for care.

Inefficient organizations, ones that get too little
mileage out of the money they spend, pose a second problem. Public schools are widely acknowledged to fall into
this category. *Business Week* reported in 1995 that while
inflation-adjusted expenditures on each student have
risen by 25% over the past ten years, performance measures for students have barely budged. And only 52 cents
of every dollar spent in a typical large school system
makes it into the classroom. Some national charities also
display inefficiency by, for example, spending too much
on fund-raising and administration and devoting less
than 50% of their income to services for clients.

A third difficulty is that of *private inurement*, in
which individuals who control tax-exempt organizations
attain excessive benefits for themselves. Inurement goes
beyond inefficient use of funds. When managers,
employees, or board members use resources for their
own benefit instead of for the organization's charitable
purpose, it is outright abuse. Consider Empire Blue
Cross and Blue Shield, a mammoth organization that
provides health insurance for millions of people. In one

particularly outrageous example, Empire invested $17 million in start-up funds with a dentist on its board to develop a desperately needed information system for the organization—despite the dentist's lack of experience in this field.

Salary levels in the nonprofit arena have also come into question. Undoubtedly, many executives at non-profits are worth their pay (and perhaps even more), but the American people appear to hold them to a different standard. Thus the public is likely to be incensed when it reads, as it did in a *1995 U.S. News & World Report* story, that six executives of nonprofits each earned more than $1 million in compensation.

Empire Blue Cross exposed its policyholders to excessive risk.

Problems of inurement occur in governmental organizations, too, through patronage and other means. For example, the investment bank Lazard Frères found that the government officials who select investment banks to manage their profitable $1.2 trillion municipal bond offerings were quite susceptible to "donations." Political back-scratching ultimately cost Lazard Frères and Merrill Lynch a record $24 million to settle charges brought by the Securities and Exchange Commission and a number of local governments.

A fourth kind of problem develops when organizations take on *excessive risk*. When Orange County's former treasurer borrowed some $16 billion to invest in speculative securities, he was using highly variable sources of revenue to meet budgeted interest and payroll expenses—a recipe that would eventually lead to financial disaster. And Empire Blue Cross exposed its policyholders to excessive risk by running its reserves down to 0.6% of revenues, in violation of the 8.0% mandated by the New York State Department of Insurance.

These problems can become especially severe because nonprofits and governments lack the three basic accountability mechanisms of business. First, they do not have the self-interest that comes with ownership and helps to ensure that managers do not receive excessive compensation, that the business accomplishes its goals efficiently, and that risks are appropriately evaluated. Second, they often lack the competition that would force efficiency. Many are near-monopolies, such as the public schools, or serve indigent clients who cannot shop for better services. Finally, they lack the ultimate barometer of business success, the profit measure. Although profits are not as relevant to organizations whose primary purpose is to improve society, alternative measures of performance are hard to find.

The Board of Supervisors failed to heed warnings about Orange County's financial condition.

To some extent, elections for government officials and the oversight of the board of directors in nonprofit organizations compensate for the absence of these accountability mechanisms. But in the case of government, the meaning of election results can be difficult to interpret. For example, the question of why the Republican Party regained control of the U.S. House of Representatives in 1994 after 40 years of Democratic rule will be debated for years to come. Contrast this ambiguity with the clarity of the message received by U.S. automobile manufacturers after they lost billions of dollars to competitors.

Further, members of a nonprofit's board and leaders in government cannot always compensate for the absence of owners, customer choice, and a profit measure. The United Way of America's board, for example, was studded with *Fortune* 500 CEOs who were fully informed about the compensation and perquisites granted their president. And Orange County's Board of Supervisors failed to heed the accurate, dire warnings about the county's fragile financial condition.

The Foundation for New Era Philanthropy, based in Radnor, Pennsylvania, managed to fool the best and the brightest in what was essentially a Ponzi scheme. New Era's executive director promised that every dollar given him by charitable organizations and philanthropists would be matched by equal donations from anonymous donors. When he finally confessed that those donors didn't exist, between $175 million and $225 million was missing. He had received contributions from luminaries of American business and journalism, including Laurence Rockefeller and ABC News anchor Peter Jennings, who had been introduced to the fund through friends in cozy social networks. Tough-minded investigations of New Era's finances were in short supply because, as the ex-prosecutor mayor of Philadelphia (whose institutions were a particular target) later admitted, New Era's executive director "seemed to be a wonderful guy."

The people serving on New Era's and other boards are talented and devoted, but they are simply too few in number to replicate the valuable diversity of opinion provided by customers. And no matter how devoted they are, their scrutiny is unlikely to be as intense as an owner's.

One Solution: DADS (Disclosure, Analysis, Dissemination, Sanctions)

The U.S. Congress, the SEC, and the Department of the Treasury have made recent, laudable efforts to shed more light on governmental and nonprofit organizations, but their attempts stop short of lifting the veil of secrecy. I would like to propose a potentially powerful remedy that I call DADS: Increase the *disclosure, analysis*, and *dissemination* of information on the performance of nonprofit and governmental organizations, and apply *sanctions* against those that do not comply with these requirements.

Can such simple measures to increase the quality of information really help? Considerable evidence supports their efficacy. The information dug up by an enterprising reporter curtailed the criminal wrongdoings of the former president of the United Way of America. Analyses conducted by persistent accountants derailed the New Era scam and exposed the excessive risk in Orange County's strategy. An NAACP board member noted that "public embarrassment" spurred the organization to replace its chairman after published articles accused him of improperly spending $1.4 million of its money. As future U.S. Supreme Court justice Louis Brandeis noted in 1913, "Publicity is justly commended as a remedy for social and industrial diseases. Sunlight is said to be the best of disinfectants."

The DADS remedy for the lack of accountability mechanisms in nonprofits and governments takes as its template the requirements put forth by the SEC for businesses whose securities fall under its jurisdiction. Like any code of conduct, the rules of the SEC have at times been flouted and circumnavigated, as in the trading and investment banking scandals of the 1980s and 1990s. But the commission has proved remarkably capable of reining in and preventing the kinds of abuses that plague nonprofit organizations and governments. (See the insert "A Useful Analogy: The Origin of the SEC," on page 19.) The SEC's success derives from the totality of its efforts, each of which complements the others: Disclosure is ineffective without analysis; both are to no avail without dissemination; and all three may fail without sanctions. A deeper look at the four pillars of DADS will help clarify why they are needed.

DISCLOSURE

Currently there is little disclosure of performance information for nonprofit and governmental organizations, especially measures of effectiveness such as client satisfaction. Financial information is often lacking as well. Although the Internal Revenue Service requires financial statements and some compensation and outcome disclosure from exempt organizations in an annual return called Form 990, the disclosure has been of such poor quality that the attorney general of Connecticut found that two-thirds of the forms filed contained at least one arithmetic error. The U.S. General Accounting Office found that half of those they reviewed were missing at least one of the required supporting schedules.

Unlike the annual reports of publicly traded corporations, financial statements of nonprofits and governments do not always conform to generally accepted accounting principles (GAAP), nor have they always been audited by a third party following generally accepted auditing standards. Even the most basic information may be absent. The bankrupt District of Columbia government, for example, has such poor records that estimates of its cash balances for year-end 1995 ranged from positive $50 million to negative $350 million. And poor records made it impossible to determine how many children were enrolled in the district's public schools.

ANALYSIS

The little information that does exist about the perform-ance of nonprofits and governments is rarely analyzed. Analysis is difficult because counterparts to the financial ratios and other techniques widely used to evaluate business performance barely exist for nonprofits and governments. The excellent performance standards of the National Charities Information Bureau and the Council of Better Business Bureau's Philanthropic Advi-sory Service are applied to only a limited number of charities. With the exception of the special studies conducted by organizations such as the General Accounting Office, important questions about the effectiveness and efficiency of nonprofit organizations and governments routinely go unasked.

The sheer quantity of financial data provided by government can discourage analysis.

Other factors can complicate analysis. Because the process of allocating joint costs to particular functions is very complex, organizations may arrive at vastly differ-ent cost estimates for substantially equivalent activities. For example, some nonprofits may classify a portion of their fund-raising expenses as program services to their clients. The use of different methods makes it hard to compare organizations, and it may obscure knowledge of where their money actually goes.

Finally, the sheer quantity of financial data provided by governments sometimes precludes analysis. For example, the voluminous contents of Orange County's inch-thick *1993 Annual Financial Report* no doubt defused the enthusiasm of many potential readers and caused them to miss the forest for the trees.

DISSEMINATION

The dissemination of information is also meager. Organizations apparently breach with some frequency the U.S. tax code provision permitting access to their 990 forms and other IRS filings. Testifying in 1993, the attorney general of Texas noted that in his experience "it usually takes months for the IRS to respond to a request for a Form 990, and [sometimes] the IRS has been unable to locate a requested form." Ordinary citizens have even worse luck. No clearinghouse exists for disseminating material information about nonprofits. Nor is the IRS allowed to disclose the reasons for its revocation of an organization's tax exemption or for other adverse actions.

Governments are notoriously slow in disseminating needed information as well. Even the election candidate opposing Orange County's treasurer could not obtain detailed descriptions of how the county's multibillion-dollar portfolio was invested until shortly before the election—and even then, he obtained them only through California's Freedom of Information Act.

SANCTIONS

Publicly owned companies that fail to disclose, analyze, and disseminate required information face sanctions by the SEC. Penalties include the imposition of fines and the issuance of cease-and-desist orders. The SEC's power to sanction has helped ensure that high-quality information flows from businesses to the public. No comparable sanctions exist for nonprofit and governmental organizations.

Although the SEC can punish dealers of municipal securities, it cannot compel the issuing governments themselves to provide additional information or analysis. In the case of nonprofits, the IRS is the main sanctioning agency, having the power to revoke a nonprofit institution's tax-exempt status. But to do so is akin to capital punishment, and the sanction is seldom applied. The enforcement efforts of the IRS are focused on areas related to the agency's tax administration objectives, such as the conduct of unrelated businesses and excessive compensation, and on fundamental reassessments of the basis for tax exemptions. The problems of ineffectiveness, inefficiency, and risk are not likely to be reviewed by the IRS.

The IRS can inflict capital punishment on a nonprofit by revoking its tax-exempt status.

At the state level, the attorneys general have broad authority to represent the public interest regarding charitable funds. Concern about deceptive solicitation practices has led most states to require registration of charitable organizations. In general, the states seem to believe, as does Congress, that accountability for nonprofits is provided by reliance on donations. But can the public really make informed choices without better information?

DADS in Practice

How would DADS operate for governmental and nonprofit organizations? First off, they would be required to disclose their financial statements. To ensure greater comparability than now exists, they should be required to follow GAAP, as articulated by the Financial and Governmental Accounting Standards Boards (FASB and GASB), in reports to their donors and taxpayers.

This recommendation, however, will only partially remedy the problems. For one thing, there are holes in GAAP. (See the insert "The Gaps in GAAP.") Moreover, accounting measures are primarily limited to those events that can be described in monetary terms. But disclosure of nonfinancial quantitative measures of performance is uniquely important for nonprofits and governments. How else will readers know whether an organization is fulfilling its mission?

For example, although expenses are important indicators of a business's use of resources, they do not capture the value of the dedicated Americans who volunteer in nonprofits; nor do they measure the results of their services. And the accounting measure of revenues ignores the subsidizing of prices by nonprofits and governments for indigent users. A low level of revenues might indicate disaster in a business and success in a social enterprise.

Without information, the public can't know if an organization is fulfilling its mission.

Measures should include the quantity and quality of services provided by the organization. For example, a nonprofit hospital might report the number of open-heart surgeries it performed; the quality of the procedures as indicated by the rates of mortality and morbidity in comparison to similar hospitals; and an assessment of the number of uninsured and fully insured patients treated. Similarly, a school system might reveal the number of eleventh-grade students enrolled; how they performed on standard achievement tests in comparison to students at similar schools; and how many of the students have special education needs. Measures of client satisfaction are very important, too, especially for

monopoly or near-monopoly organizations. (Although it
is difficult to obtain such measures, early results from the
"report cards" produced by some health care organizations and the measurement efforts supported by the
GASB are encouraging.)

The public also should be fully informed about executive compensation at comparable organizations. Disclosure of information about service results and compensation would allow people to evaluate whether an
organization is achieving its objectives and to compare
its achievements and costs with those of similar organizations.

A "management discussion and analysis" (MD&A)
report should be issued at least annually. The SEC speci-
fies the topics to be covered in corporate MD&A reports
to ensure substance and comparability. The four questions posed in my article "Effective Oversight: A Guide
for Nonprofit Directors" (HBR, July–August 1994) can
provide a starting point for the MD&A content for nonprofits and governments. If those questions had been
asked, the problems in Orange County could have been
exposed. (See the insert "Early Warning Signals.")

Publicly traded corporations are required to send
annual reports and proxy statements to their stockholders, and many send quarterly reports as well. Corporate
CEOs typically address open annual meetings of the
stockholders, and SEC filings can be accessed easily
through on-line services. Nonprofit and governmental
organizations should follow the corporate model and
report to their stakeholders—the donors and taxpayers
who fund their efforts. Information should be widely dis-
seminated and easily obtained.

Finally, some form of sanctions is required. As is the
case for corporations, it seems likely that the federal gov-

ernment would provide the most effective enforcement of these reporting requirements. Federal oversight would eliminate the uneven regulation of organizations that now exists at the state level. Given its role in sanctioning dealers of municipal securities, the SEC seems an obvious choice to enforce DADS in municipalities. Without instituting new rules, it could require issuers of municipal debt to provide timely annual reports to the marketplace; however, the SEC would require new authority to set standards for accounting and other disclosures.

But the SEC is not a natural choice for nonprofit organizations, because they do not issue securities. The focus of the IRS on tax administration makes it an imperfect candidate for the job, but given its history of oversight of nonprofits, it may still be the best-suited of all existing agencies.

Granting the authority to impose sanctions would raise important constitutional issues. The Tenth Amendment strictly limits the powers of the federal government over state and local governments. And nonprofits have triumphed in First Amendment lawsuits against government officials who tried to apply standards to fund-raising activities. The choice of enforcement agencies, if the principle of sanctions is accepted, should be a matter of considerable public debate. Once

After Orange County's bankruptcy, voters refused to raise taxes until the county slashed its budget.

chosen, these agencies should then turn to a group modeled after the independent, privately funded accounting standard-setting organizations, such as the FASB, to develop specific disclosure requirements. Experience has shown that such private organizations are appropriately responsive to their constituencies.

Developing appropriate sanctions will also require thoughtful debate. Sanctions could range from sunset provisions, which would require review of an organization's tax-exempt status on a periodic basis, to increased civil or criminal penalties for managers and board members who fail to comply with reporting and disclosure requirements. Board members and overseers could also be asked to take a more active role by signing off on the proposed MD&A and other required reports. But it will be important to consider the fairness and practicality of requiring the largely unpaid members of the boards of nonprofits or the minimally compensated elected officials of many small government units to shoulder yet more legal liability. Perhaps wide public disclosure of wrongdoing is a sufficiently strong sanction. For example the mere disclosure of its problems was sufficient cause for the NAACP to oust its leaders.

Improved Efficiency, Renewed Public Confidence

Will the public really be interested in such information and capable of acting on it? Indeed it will. After all, the average U.S. family pays more in taxes than for food eaten at home, and Americans donate billions of dollars and hours of service to charities. They also respond to information. It is surely no accident that total giving to local United Ways has yet to equal the levels it reached before news of the scandal involving the United Way of America's president broke. Similarly, after Orange County's bankruptcy, newly informed voters refused to raise taxes until the county government slashed its bloated budget.

Virtually every group that has opposed disclosure has contended that the dissemination of information is not a good solution because the public won't be able to understand the published information. That argument holds little merit. If understanding is a problem, then nonprofits and governments need to improve the clarity of the information. The public funds these organizations and deserves a clear accounting of how its money is spent.

I believe that implementation of DADS will increase contributions to nonprofit organizations in the same way that securities laws helped to create a large, efficient capital market. DADS will enhance donors' confidence that their support will be used for worthy causes rather than for private inurement or the pursuit of ill-conceived ventures. It may also diminish the quantity of funds squandered on troubled institutions and redirect money to more productive uses. Thus the overall economic impact of DADS may be to increase revenues for nonprofits, and perhaps even for governments, while improving their efficiency.

But DADS cannot be put into effect without incurring new costs. Organizations that currently do not follow GAAP or collect information about the results of their activities may face substantial new expenses. For that reason, the many small but important nonprofit organizations should be given special consideration. On the other hand, dissemination costs are likely to be minor because of the extensive mailings that most nonprofits and governments already carry out.

The major costs for implementing DADS may occur as organizations answer the four questions in the insert "Early Warning Signals." Although these efforts probably will not require additional out-of-pocket expenses, they will nevertheless demand considerable time from top management. Many organizations may well have avoided answering these questions in the past because they raise awkward, difficult issues about their fundamental purpose and methods: Who are we? What should we be doing? How well are we doing? These are among the painful, introspective questions that most organizations, like most people, prefer to leave unasked. But they must be answered sooner or later. All too frequently, they are addressed only when an organization faces major problems. The analytic component of DADS will force recalcitrant organizations to address these issues before disaster strikes.

Nonprofit and governmental organizations support the most important aspects of our lives. When these institutions fail, the breach of public trust is devastating. Just as the SEC rules were grounded in promoting investor confidence, we need similar guidelines for the nonprofit and government sectors to promote both donor and voter confidence.

DADS can increase public trust. But implementing it will require considerable effort. Managers and overseers of nonprofits and governments should guide and assist this process. Members of the public must show interest in the newly provided information. And elected officials need to pass the legislation that will create accountability. Without these efforts, we will undoubtedly see more debacles—such as those that devastated Orange County and the United Way—in these institutions, the most important in our society.

A Useful Analogy: The Origin of the SEC

IN CERTAIN KEY RESPECTS, the practices of nonprofit and governmental organizations today are similar to those of industrial corporations before the enactment of the Securities and Exchange Acts of 1933 and 1934. Thus the history of U.S. capital markets can help us understand the potential impact of DADS on nonprofits and governments.

During the nineteenth and early twentieth centuries, corporate America was characterized by a tradition of secrecy inherited from the days when businesses were essentially privately owned. Investors were expected to rely on the integrity of investment bankers and managers rather than on information about the business. Only meager information was presented to stockholders, and even that was provided erratically. For example, the Westinghouse Electric and Manufacturing Company neither published an annual report nor held an annual meeting from 1897 to 1905. Government did little to persuade corporations to be more forthcoming.

In the absence of public information requirements, rapacious corporate chieftains extracted huge rewards for their insider knowledge, sometimes using money supplied by an unknowing public. For example, in 1929, the head of the Chase National Bank engineered a $6.6 million loan from the bank for one of his personal holding companies to cover his short sales of Chase stock. In other words, he bet that the stock of the company he managed would decline—using the deposits of Chase customers to finance the unsavory transaction—and ultimately profited to the tune of $4 million.

When the stock market crashed in 1929 and the country fell into a massive economic depression, stories like that did grave damage to the public's confidence in the fairness of the system. In response, the U.S. Congress passed legislation in 1934 that created the Securities and Exchange Commission to regulate the disclosure, analysis, and dissemination of information for many corporate securities and the markets in which they are traded. The SEC was granted broad rule-making authority to develop the regulations and armed with the sanctions to enforce them.

The SEC has been admirably restrained in utilizing its powers, sometimes preferring to work cooperatively with various professional groups in discharging its responsibilities. For example, although it was granted the authority to establish accounting rules, the SEC made it clear from the beginning that it expected the private sector to assume the major responsibility for developing those rules. This role is carried out currently by the Financial Accounting Standards Board.

There is little doubt that the SEC has created a flow of useful data. So-called efficient market research demonstrates that the prices of publicly traded securities fully reflect this information; thus the securities of unproductive, ineffective, or reckless companies lose value. Both good news and bad become public quickly and elicit an appropriate response. Moreover, if material information is improperly withheld from the public, the SEC can come down on the offender with guns blazing.

The accountability mechanisms outlined in DADS are likely to improve the market for nonprofit and governmental organizations, some of which now behave with the same secrecy as public corporations once did. DADS would certainly increase public trust in these organizations and probably improve their performance as well.

The GAPS in GAAP

FOR NONPROFITS AND GOVERNMENTS, there are some major gaps in generally accepted accounting principles. In governmental organizations, the principles rarely include accrual accounting. For example, governments routinely omit depreciation of fixed assets in most of their financial statements. The U.S. government presents a particularly hard case: It uses cash accounting and has never produced financial statements based on the records of federal agencies. As a result, financial disclosures that could profoundly affect the country's future are ignored, such as the $12 trillion estimated in 1995 as the unfunded Social Security liability. (GASB proposals to adopt a financial reporting model are currently being discussed.)

Although GAAP for nonprofit organizations have recently been updated with Financial Accounting Standards 116 and 117, issued by the FASB, these standards fail to fix all the gaps in the nonprofit GAAP. For example, museums can safely omit most of the value of their collections—usually their most precious asset and the core of their mission—from their financial statements. And a government-operated hospital or school can continue to produce financial statements that use a different version of GAAP from those produced by a private nonprofit hospital or school.

The new statements have also failed to require that nonprofits produce a statement of operations. As a result, one cannot ascertain the answer to a fundamental question: Do operating revenues cover operating expenses? Readers of the statements need an explanation of the components of operating income so they can distinguish among normal, recurring, and other types of revenues and expenses. For example, Boston's Museum of Science classifies ánnual-fund gifts in operations because management views such gifts as a reliable and renewable basis of support for the museum's operations. But if the museum receives an unusually large annual gift, museum officials will call the donor to determine if it is likely to recur. If not, they classify the gift among nonoperating revenues.

When these gaps in GAAP are corrected, the usefulness of the financial statements of nonprofits and governments will be enhanced considerably.

Early Warning Signals

MOST OBSERVERS WERE TAKEN BY SURPRISE when prosperous Orange County, California, declared bankruptcy in 1994. Could this debacle have been averted? Would answering the following four basic questions have provided early warning signs? With these questions in mind, I revisited the county's 1993 financial statements armed with only a $3.99 solar-powered calculator.

Are the organization's goals consistent with its financial resources? The answer to this question should enable the reader to judge the entity's effectiveness (did the organization reach its goals?), efficiency (how much money did it use to attain them?), and level of inurement (how much was spent on the board and top management versus other important functions?). Unfortunately, Orange County's annual report contains absolutely no information in all its 204 pages about what it accomplished with the billions of dollars it spent. Measures of the safety, health, and welfare of its citizens are not provided; neither are efficiency measures. Executive compensation is not disclosed. Did the county spend more or less on public protection than similar jurisdictions? *I can't say.*

The annual report does have enough data to judge how the county's financial structure matched its goals. In plain English, did it have enough money to survive?

Short-term liquidity measures, such as the current ratio (the ratio of current assets that can be quickly liquidated to current liabilities), help one to judge whether the organization's mission is matched by an appropriate level of resources. Organizations with high current ratios are like the proverbial rich widows or widowers of the nonprofit and government sectors, who horde piles of current assets without using them to achieve worthwhile social goals. Conversely, organizations with low current ratios are likely to be profligate spenders whose appetites exceed their means.

But the Orange County balance sheet did not classify assets and liabilities as current or noncurrent. Digging deeper, and subtracting $420 million in long-term debt from $13.8 billion of liabilities, we can infer that current liabilities were approximately $13.4 billion. To repay those obligations, the county owned approximately $15.4 billion of securities whose market value fluctuated with interest rates. If interest rates were to rise, as they subsequently did, the value of the securities would fall. (Indeed, if the securities turned out to be sufficiently exotic, they may not have been able to find any market at all; thus their owners would have been forced to hold them until they matured.) The average term of $7.5 billion of these assets was approximately 2.5 years. If we infer that this portion of the portfolio consisted of securities with maturities evenly distributed between one and five years, then only $1.5 billion (20% of $7.5 billion) would mature in the following year. Adding that figure to the remaining

$7.9 billion ($15.4 minus $7.5) yields available assets of $9.4 billion, which left Orange County with negative working capital of $4 billion.

Not great news, but couldn't the county just keep rolling over the liabilities? Yes, as long as it could afford the interest expense. But could it? In 1993, as the financial statements show, the county experienced a deficit of $86 million. And because government accounting is darn close to cash accounting, this deficit is a real cash drain. So if Orange County were to run at a deficit again or if the interest-sensitive assets were to decline in value—pull the plug, it's all over.

But that's not all. On page 162 of the report, we read of the mysterious addition of $25.6 billion in assets and a deduction of $21.8 billion from the county's agency fund, which accounted for the moneys that other governmental organizations had invested in the Orange County pool. Not a word of explanation accompanies the movement of these billions of dollars.

These mystery moneys were key to Orange County's downfall. As California's state auditor later explained to a congressional committee, the treasurer used the original $7.5 billion as collateral to build up a portfolio of $20.6 billion—all of it financed by debt. Further, he invested up to 32% of that sum in "inverse floaters," whose yield varies in the opposite direction of interest rate movements. His bet that interest rates would decrease, when in fact they increased, was central to this megadisaster. Not only did the yield on the floaters head south, but the value of the fixed-interest securities he had used to collateralize the loans also diminished. A bad double play.

But, even absent this information, the unexplained movement of billions of dollars sounds an alarm. If the $15.4 billion discussed above raised a concern, these additional billions just upped the ante. Although I cannot judge the county's effectiveness and efficiency, I can reasonably conclude that its government is no rich widow or widower. Its financial resources seem barely adequate to enable it to achieve its goals.

Is the organization practicing intergenerational equity? This jawbreaker is meant to judge whether we, the present generation, treat future generations fairly, leaving them some assets and not a big pile of debts. I proposed to evaluate intergenerational equity with a measure called the inflation-adjusted fund balance. (The fund balance is roughly equivalent to owners' equity in corporations and will be called *net assets* in future statements by nonprofits.) If this figure remains the same over the course of time, then the present generation will have neither depleted nor added to the owners' stake in the organization's assets. Whether it is desirable to maintain value depends on the organization, of course.

In the absence of major increases in productivity or changes in mission, a government in a growing area like Orange County should probably increase—but not excessively—its inflation-adjusted fund balance so that it can provide the same level of services, per capita, over time. Although this measure cannot be computed because the annual report lacks depreciation and inflationary measures, the inflation-adjusted fund balance certainly increased during 1993. For example, given a 3% rate of inflation, the county's $1.4 billion of fixed assets should have increased by $52 million just to stay even; instead, the county spent $228 million on capital outlays.

Orange County appears to be adding to its infrastructure at a very fast rate. Future generations will need to pay for this furious construction of additional infrastructure. Did they really need it?

Are the sources and uses of funds appropriately matched? Who would finance the purchase of a house with a loan that comes due next year? Apparently the former treasurer of Orange County would. Whereas the rest of us would finance the purchase of a long-term asset with a long-term liability—like a mortgage—he financed the purchase of billions of dollars of longer-term assets with short-term liabilities, thereby mismatching the sources and uses of funds. Further, he matched fixed expenses with variable revenues, a strategy akin to financing the payment of a home mortgage (fixed expense) with earnings from the stock market (variable revenue).

Short and long, fixed and variable—these two mismatches put Orange County in substantial jeopardy, all the more so because of the enormous magnitude of the sums involved.

Is the organization sustainable? The adage "Don't put all your eggs in one basket" provides good financial advice, too. Diversification is correlated with sustainability because if one aspect of a strategy fails, another can succeed.

Orange County's finances were underdiversified in many ways. The county was highly dependent on moneys earned by its investments. Too much of its capital came from debt, and ultimately, too much of its money was spent to repay it. And the large concentration of interest-sensitive assets on its balance sheet was likely to diminish in value at some time because of the uncertainty of interest rates.

In this case, consideration of the four questions could have provided strong warnings about Orange County's narrow margin of liquidity and high level of risk. A management discussion and analysis report can do the same for other nonprofits and governments by providing early warning signals about ineffective, inefficient, and reckless organizations.

Originally published in March–April 1996
Reprint 96207

The author wishes to acknowledge the help of the following members of the Harvard Business School community: Jeffrey Cronin of Research Services, research associate Ann Winslow, Professor Joseph Hinsey IV, and the Social Enterprise Interest Group. She is also grateful for the assistance of John Moorlach, treasurer of Orange County, California.

H. David Sherman, an associate professor at Northeastern University's College of Business Administration in Boston, Massachusetts, coauthored "The Gaps in GAAP" insert.

Effective Oversight

A Guide for Nonprofit Directors

REGINA E. HERZLINGER

Executive Summary

MORE THAN EVER, the public is looking to the nonprofit sector to address the pressing social problems that are hobbling the United States. Nonprofits have a record of promoting literacy, providing health care, supporting the arts, and offering a safety net for the poor that neither business nor government can match.

But, as Regina Herzlinger observes in this article inaugurating HBR's Social Enterprise department, recent revelations suggest that nonprofits are far from faultless. Some have come under fire in recent years for rewarding executives with the kind of salaries and perks once reserved for corporate heavyweights. Other organizations, such as hospitals, have been charged with providing too few services for the poor.

As a result of such revelations about some nonprofits, *all* nonprofits face increased scrutiny from both benefac-

tors and government regulators. To survive under this spot-
light, a nonprofit needs a powerful and proactive board
of directors to provide oversight. The board must assume
the roles played in a business by owners and the market,
ensuring that the nonprofit accomplishes its mission efficiently and devising its own system of measurement and
control. Herzlinger proposes four questions to help board
members create such a system: (1) Are the organization's
goals consistent with its financial resources? (2) Is the
organization practicing intergenerational equity? (3) Are
the sources and uses of funds appropriately matched? (4)
Is the organization sustainable?

Together these questions offer a framework to help
board members provide the critical oversight that nonprofits need to survive.

 M ORE THAN EVER, the public is looking to the
nonprofit sector to address the social problems that
are hobbling the United States—problems that business and government have failed to solve. Nonprofit
organizations hold more promise than businesses do,
because they are rela-
tively free of the unre-
lenting need to increase
profits, which so often
results in a compro-
mised quality of ser-
vices. And, unlike gov-
ernment agencies,
nonprofits are directly accountable to their boards of
directors and to the contributors on whose support
they depend. But to flourish in an economy that

*After the Christian Science
Church lost $325 million in
its electronic media
ventures, some constituents
called for the board to
resign.*

demands increased organizational efficiency and in a society that demands increased accountability, nonprofits need powerful and proactive boards of directors to provide oversight. And those boards need to devise systems of measurement and control.

Nonprofits have a record of promoting literacy, providing health care, supporting the arts, and offering a safety net for the poor that neither business nor government can match. New York City even recruited the nonprofit Salvation Army to run some of its shelters for the homeless—shelters the homeless cite for efficient operations and compassionate workers. But nonprofits can also stumble, as recent revelations about abuses of funds and organizational inefficiency suggest.

Some organizations have rewarded executives with the kind of salaries and perks once reserved for corporate heavyweights. The public was shocked, for example, by the 1992 disclosure that the president of the United Way earned $463,000 per year—while the average U.S. family got by on $36,000. Meanwhile, tuition at nonprofit colleges grew by more than twice the general rate of inflation between 1980 and 1990. And then there was the well-publicized attempt by the Christian Science Church to diversify, resulting in a $325 million loss and prompting some constituents to call for the resignation of the board.

Other nonprofits, such as hospitals, have been charged with providing too few services, particularly to the poor, who should be their primary concern. A 1987 *Harvard Business Review* article concluded that the nonprofit hospital chains studied did not provide sufficient charity care to warrant their exemption from paying income taxes.[1] Indeed, the poor would have benefited more if the considerable profits earned by those so-called nonprofit hospitals had been taxed and the proceeds used to pay for their hospital care. In 1989, a General Accounting Office study confirmed this controversial conclusion when it reported that 57% of the nonprofit hospitals it examined provided charity care whose value was less than the tax benefits they received. And today, state and local governments are likely to sue nonprofit hospitals for tax payments when they provide inadequate levels of charity care.

As a result of such revelations about some nonprofits, *all* nonprofits face increased scrutiny from both benefactors and government regulators. And the role of the board member has become that much more critical. Most board members take seriously their legal responsibility to act with care and good faith, but they don't always know how to translate their life experiences into effective oversight of these unique organizations. Traditional measures of corporate performance, such as profits or return on investment, are hardly relevant.

Nonprofits lack the guidance the market provides corporations. The reactions of clients to the products and services that nonprofits offer are not as revealing as the responses of customers to the products and services sold by a for-profit company. Because nonprofits are usually subsidized and their services are frequently free, clients are more likely to forgive poor quality and ignore inefficiency. Consequently, board members cannot rely on a key indicator of corporate success—the value of services sold—to evaluate their organization's performance. Market signals may also mislead when nonprofits provide innovative services that are intended to shape public opinion rather than appeal to the masses. If patrons fail to throng to an avant-garde art exhibition but critics find it provocative, a museum may well have accomplished its goal.

Board members of nonprofits may also be perplexed about their appropriate roles. Some are so intimidated by the talent and professional expertise of the organization's employees that they abandon their oversight role. How can I tell a symphony orchestra how to play Beethoven? they ask themselves. How can I tell a doctor how to operate? At the opposite end of the spectrum are the enthusiastic amateurs who become excessively involved in the organization's work. Such board members may give unsolicited—and unwanted—counsel on orchestra programs, museum exhibitions, educational curricula, surgical and diagnostic protocols, or social service intervention strategies. Other overseers pour themselves into fund-raising, perceiving their mission solely in terms of securing the organization's financial welfare. Finally, some board members use their appointment to add a notch on their social-climbing belt. Events planned ostensibly to help the organization are actually vehicles for enhancing a board member's status.

But the role of a director is neither to counsel conductors nor to climb on their coattails. Goals like fund-raising are important but ultimately secondary to the primary mission of overseeing the organization. If the board of a nonprofit is to be effective, it must assume the roles that owners and the market play in business. The board must ensure that the nonprofit's mission is appropriate to its charitable orientation and that it accomplishes that mission efficiently. In the absence of concrete measures and market signals about mission, quality, and efficiency, that is no easy task. Consequently, the board must devise its own system of measurement and control.

Based on studies of hundreds of nonprofit organizations during the last 25 years, I have developed four questions that can help board members create such a system:

1. Are the organization's goals consistent with its financial resources?

2. Is the organization practicing intergenerational equity?

3. Are the sources and uses of funds appropriately matched?

4. Is the organization sustainable? Together these questions can offer a framework to help board members provide the critical oversight that nonprofit organizations need in order to survive.

W HEN THE FORMER EXECUTIVE director of the Girl Scouts of the U.S.A., Frances Hesselbein, assumed her position in 1976, she found an organization with substantial strengths: membership in the millions; a devoted, skilled executive staff and volunteers, most of whom had been Scouts in their youth; and numerous camp properties. The Girl Scouts' historic mission of providing girls with opportunities to define their identities, bond with other females, and identify more closely with nature was consistent with the emerging feminist and environmental movements of the time.

But the organization was also showing signs of strain: membership was declining; some individual councils were operating with small but steady losses; some camps were underutilized and poorly maintained; and the organization was increasingly dependent on the sale of its famous cookies as a source of revenue. Hesselbein realized that the trend of steady, small losses would ultimately deny Girl Scout services to future generations of girls, that an excessive investment in camping properties would reduce the councils' ability to provide other kinds of services, and that over-reliance on cookie sales as a source of revenue would expose the councils to great financial risk if sales declined. Her observations form the heart of the four questions.

When she asked whether there were too many camps, she was questioning whether the councils' *goals and financial resources were consistent*. For example, if only 10% of a council's middle-class members attended a camp, should the council devote a larger percentage of its expenses and assets to subsidizing them? In many cases, the councils concluded that the answer was no and reluctantly dispatched camping properties that had been the source of fond memories for many of their adult members but were no longer an appropriate use of the organization's resources.

When the councils lost money in their yearly operations, they were most likely depriving future Girl Scouts of the benefits received by the present generation. That kind of loss results in a lack of *intergenerational equity*— a jaw-breaking term that means "fairness in dealing with future generations." Because many of the people who served on the boards of the councils were former Scouts, they found this issue compelling. At Hesselbein's urging, they acted to reverse their losses, insisting that their councils break even or generate profits.

When some councils analyzed their activities, they found that although most of their expenses were fixed, such as those of operating the camps and paying their executive staffs, a sizable portion of their revenues was variable and outside their control. The amount of a United Way grant to a local council, for example, could not be antici-

Frances Hesselbein helped some Girl Scout councils change from organizations that were losing money into ones with sound fiscal practices and a bright future.

pated. Furthermore, the revenues the councils did control, such as those from membership and camping fees, did not cover their fixed expenses. It was hardly surprising that some camp properties were run-down. Hesselbein saw that there was a clear *mismatch between the sources and uses of funds.* Some councils corrected the mismatch by increasing their fixed revenues and the proportion of their variable expenses. They increased membership and hired temporary employees, for example, if fixed revenues were not available to match the fixed expenses of permanent staff.

Hesselbein observed that councils that concentrated a large proportion of their resources in any one activity put their *sustainability* in jeopardy. For example, a council that derived the bulk of its revenues from cookie sales would be in serious trouble if cookie sales declined. (One year sales did plummet after unsubstantiated reports circulated that some cookies contained pins.) Similarly, the future of a council whose assets were invested primarily in camping properties would be in jeopardy if camping waned in popularity or if the areas abutting camps were turned into dumping grounds. The many councils that acted to diversify their activities greatly increased their chances of survival.

ALTHOUGH NONPROFIT ORGANIZATIONS lack
many of the concrete measures and market signals that
for-profit corporations enjoy, there are key indicators
on which boards of directors can rely. Answering the
four questions can help nonprofits develop such measures. (See "Selected Indicators for Answering the Four
Questions.")

**Are the organization's goals consistent with its
financial resources?** Many organizations have excessively modest goals relative to their resources. Nonprofit
charitable foundations control vast assets of approximately $120 billion. But their assets have grown much
faster than the amounts they give away. For example,
while the Robert Wood Johnson Foundation's investment holdings have tripled since 1981, its grants have
grown by only 9%. In 1990, with assets of $2.6 billion, it
spent $130 million—but only $66 million of that was in
grants, according to Gilbert M. Gaul and Neill A.
Borowski's "Warehouses of Wealth: The Tax-Free Economy" (*Philadelphia Inquirer,* April 24, 1993).

Conversely, some nonprofits have overly ambitious
goals given their resources. For example, the directors of

Selected Indicators for Answering the Four Questions

Questions

1. Consistency between goals and financial resources	2. Intergenerational equity	3. Match between sources and uses of funds	4. Sustainability
Indicators			
1. Asset turnover; liquidity; sociodemographic characteristics of clients; distribution of expenses	2. Inflation-adjusted balance sheet	3. Analysis of controllability of fund sources and uses	4. Integrated financial and strategic plan; dispersion measures

the Christian Science Church invested $325 million in a variety of nonprint media in an effort to bring the *Christian Science Monitor* into the age of electronic journalism. The cable television venture ended in 1992, although the shortwave and radio ventures continue. Some contend that the church severely strained its resources by pumping so much money into cable.

Two ratios help measure the consistency between goals and financial resources. The asset turnover ratio measures the relationship between sales revenues and assets, and provides an indication of how much service activity (as measured in sales revenues) the assets generate. Organizations with high asset turnover are probably generating more service activity than those with low asset turnover. Low-turnover organizations are more likely to be investing their assets to earn income than to provide services. The liquidity ratio measures the relationship between assets and liabilities and also helps to determine the consistency of goals and resources. A highly liquid organization usually has overly modest social goals, whereas an organization with low liquidity may be excessively ambitious.

Both ratios must be carefully computed and cautiously interpreted. For example, neither should include assets whose use has been restricted by donors or the revenues those assets generate. For such restricted resources, the ratios should be computed separately. Similarly, the sales revenues included in the turnover ratio should be valued at their market price if prices have been discounted for indigent users.

There is no absolute right level for these ratios just as there is no one right body temperature. Ratios are meaningful only if they are interpreted in the context of similar organizations. (Industry groups publish comparative data.) A comparison of dissimilar nonprofit organizations cannot provide useful information for oversight purposes. The fact that a social service agency has an asset turnover ratio of 4, for example, while a hospital has a ratio of 1 is not particularly illuminating, because the hospital cannot achieve the ratio of the social service agency any more than an elephant can achieve the speed of a sparrow. But it is useful for directors to know that their hospital has an asset turnover ratio of 0.8 while the average for hospitals its size is 1. In this context it is not only appropriate but also useful to ask, Why is our elephant at the rear of the herd?

A museum that takes in more money from its gift shop than from admissions may lose sight of its purpose.

Directors should determine the social and demographic characteristics of the users who generate the sales revenues to ensure that the organization is serving the truly needy and the other groups it intends to serve. A hospital should track its charity patients, a school its scholarship recipients, and a museum its visitors to make sure that they are not inadvertently serving only the well-to-do.

Sometimes financial resources are not well matched with goals because they are derived or used in ways that are inconsistent with the organization's mission. When nonprofit organizations invest in subsidiary activities whose sole purpose is to generate funds to support the organization's charitable mission, such as museums that run gift shops or religious organizations that sponsor rummage sales, those activities can take on a life of their own and dominate the agenda of the organization. In the case of one prominent museum, the revenues earned from merchandising sales were reportedly 17 times higher than the revenues from admissions—an imbalance that could cause a museum to focus more on merchandising than on art.

Other fund-raising activities may also be inappropriate given the stated goals of an organization. The driving force of a nonprofit should be a desire to do good, not to serve commercial interests.

One can question, for example, the appropriateness of a public broadcasting station's airing a long statement of gratitude to a corporate sponsor. After all, the nonprofit station exists solely to provide commercial-free broadcasting, and the statement of gratitude may serve the same function as a commercial. And is it appropriate for nonprofit, tax-exempt universities to create subsidiaries like those that sell computer equipment and software, and compete with taxpaying businesses primarily on the basis of lower costs due to their tax-exempt status? Nonprofit organizations certainly were not given their tax-free status to gain an advantage in competing with tax-paying businesses.

Further problems arise when nonprofits spend money on activities and gifts that appear extravagant to the public. Some Blue Cross-Blue Shield plans—nonprofit health-insurance organizations once known for their charity—are a case in point. Last year, the *New York Times* reported that while insurance rates skyrocketed, the Maryland Blue Cross-Blue Shield plan bought a $300,000 skybox at a baseball park and the New York State plan spent $15,000 on a gift of silver punch bowls for board members—the very people responsible for making sure funds are used to advance the nonprofit's social goals.

The distribution of expenses is another important indicator of the match between resources and goals. The bulk of a nonprofit's expenses should be used to provide services, unless the organization is undertaking a massive fund drive or unusual administrative work. Too often, administrators become self-serving, permitting administrative expenses to grow while the expenses of the service component shrink. A landmark national survey by James Cook, "Charity Checklist" (*Forbes*, October 28, 1991), indicated that expenses for program services as a percentage of all nonprofit expenses averaged 76% and ranged from a high of 99% (for the Jewish Communal Fund of New York) to a low of 2%. The percentage of contributions spent on fund-raising averaged 18% and ranged from 0% (for the Jewish Communal Fund) to 90%.

Nonprofits should not sacrifice present generations of users for the benefit of future generations.

Comparative surveys can provide nonprofits with some guidance on how much to spend on administration, but, again, no magic formulas exist. While a start-up may well spend all its money on administration, a mature organization should not. Oversight of this issue requires board members to understand the costs of providing different services and the accounting methods used to compute them.

Such data are easily misunderstood, as the Girl Scouts of the U.S.A. discovered when an irate volunteer alleged that her local council was spending too much money on administration and not enough on program services. She failed to understand that the administrative expenses included salaries for people engaged directly in designing services for the Girl Scouts—from programs to teach wilderness survival skills to campaigns to promote responsible sexual practices—and in recruiting a diverse population of girls and volunteers. In fact, the program expenses for the Girl Scouts in 1992 represented 75.5% of revenues—a figure solidly within the average range for all nonprofits.

Is the organization practicing intergenerational equity? In general, nonprofits should not sacrifice present generations of users for the benefit of future ones and vice versa. When a charity saves an excessively large proportion of its resources to help future users, it denies benefits to present users. Conversely, when it consumes virtually all its assets to serve present users, it denies the benefits of the organization's services to future users.

Barring extraordinary circumstances, an established nonprofit organization whose financial resources are well matched with its goals should practice intergenerational equity by conserving its capital so that present and future generations have equivalent opportunities to benefit from its resources. (This measure excludes organizations that were created to accomplish a time-limited goal. For example, an organization created to bring benches into a city park should be dissolved when its goals are achieved and need not be concerned about intergenerational equity.)

An inflation-adjusted balance sheet provides a good financial measure of whether the goal of intergenerational equity has been achieved. If the fund balance account on the current period's balance sheet carries the same value as the previous period's inflation-adjusted account, the total capital available to the users of the organization's services (the fund balance) has neither increased nor decreased and intergenerational equity has been achieved. (Of course, new or rapidly expanding nonprofits cannot follow this principle: by their very nature, they are investing now—decreasing the resources available to present users—to benefit future users.) Maintaining intergenerational equity usually requires that the organization earn a profit sufficient to permit it to replace its net assets. In this case, *profit* is not a return to the owners but an allowance for the replacement of depleted capital.

Some people in business and government question the value of an inflation-adjusted balance sheet. They contend that it is rendered useless by the dubious assumptions it requires about replacement values. I disagree. After all, conventional financial statements are filled with assumptions about items such as pensions, depreciation, and amortization. And market values are readily available for measuring the inflation-adjusted values of monetary assets and liabilities. Of course, the replacement values assigned to real assets may be somewhat crude at times. But the valuable information that inflation accounting provides more than compensates for that.

Are the sources and uses of funds appropriately matched? Some expenses incurred by nonprofits are fixed in the sense that they are exceedingly difficult to reverse. The compensation of a tenured professor at a college is a fixed expense, as is that of a noted conductor of a symphony orchestra. Mandated expenses that cannot be controlled by the organization are also fixed, such as the obligation to provide certain kinds of retirement benefits. Other expenses are more readily reversible. Generally, those expenses are controllable and represent resources that can be easily purchased or not as the organization sees fit.

Fixed expenses should be funded by sources that can be readily controlled and that yield a fairly even stream of income over time—for example, the income from endowment capital invested in a well-diversified portfolio that, on average, yields roughly the same return over a long period of time. Uncontrollable, variable sources of capital are not a good way to fund fixed expenses.

To assess the match between sources and uses of funds, each must first be categorized as fixed or variable. The ideal match is between fixed revenues and all of an organization's expenses. If such a match is not possible, as is often the case, fixed expenses should be matched with fixed revenues and variable expenses with variable revenues.

Despite the rather obvious nature of these observations, they are frequently ignored. For example, many colleges and universities match the expense of compensating tenured professors with revenues earned from research grants. This combination of fixed expenses and variable revenues creates an unsustainable financial situation. Such poor matching caused students at Columbia and Yale to protest—with good reason—the unexpected downsizing of their universities. Similarly, a public broadcasting station that had matched the cost of building a large production complex with foundation funds that would be provided only if viewers matched them found itself near bankruptcy. Another public broadcasting station that had grown more cautiously, hiring staff only for a given new production and dismissing them if the production was not renewed for another season, was far more successful.

Poor matching of variable revenues and fixed expenses caused Columbia and Yale to downsize—and provoked student protests.

Is the organization sustainable? If the answers to the first three questions are satisfactory, the status quo of the organization can be sustained if it is maintained on an inflation-adjusted constant value. To accomplish this goal, management should prepare a strategic plan and pro forma financial statements to demonstrate that continuation of the present policies will enable the organization

Subcommittees provide the best forum for tackling the four questions.

to survive. If the organization is planning new programs, management should present a plan that discusses the separable financial consequences of each of the programs and their combined effects on the organization. The very discipline of creating a plan that integrates strategic and financial planning often identifies some activities whose impact has not yet been fully considered.

A major impediment to the sustainability of any organization is an excessive concentration on any one item—revenue sources, objects of expense, assets, or liabilities. It is startling to note how few nonprofits disperse their financial resources adequately. They become entranced with one person or project and concentrate their resources in one place. Concentration greatly increases the organization's risk. For example, revenues derived primarily from endowments invested in equities are vulnerable to stock market cycles; expenses concentrated in any one person—say, a "star" curator—are captive to that person's escalating demands; assets excessively concentrated in one category, such as a downtown campus, are subject to deterioration in value; and liabilities too heavily derived from one source—say, a savings and loan—risk the collapse of the funding resource. Dispersion in all financial categories will enhance an organization's sustainability.

IF THE ENTIRE BOARD WERE to address all four
questions, they would find the process time-consuming
and unwieldy. Subcommittees provide the best forum
for tackling the questions and determining relevant
measures and systems of control—as long as their members have the necessary credentials and experience.

Unfortunately, some nonprofit organizations place
people on boards simply because they're professionals,
they're wealthy, or they represent a particular group—
woefully inadequate criteria for board participation. Ide-
ally, board members should have "footprints"—a record
of productive involvement with the boards of other
organizations and a personal history of social service.
Potential members can be screened and trained by serving on other committees of the organization.

Board members should be willing to commit the substantial time needed to serve effectively. They should be
broadly familiar with the type of industry in which the
nonprofit operates or have operating experience at the
top levels of management. For example, a top-level executive from a company that operates budget hotels would
be a good candidate for the board of a nonprofit shelter
for the homeless.

Professionals in the actual field of endeavor of the
organization might seem like the best candidates for the
board. But many of them lack crucial managerial experience, and they may be tempted to spend too much time
second-guessing the work of the nonprofits' professionals—a role beyond the purview of the board. Professionals who are also managers, however, are often exceptional board members. A teacher who has served as a
headmaster or a physician who was a hospital CEO may

combine oversight experience with a special sensitivity to the mission of the organization. In general, board members who have track records of mentoring and development are less likely to cross the line from oversight to overmanagement.

Balance and diversity are particularly important to staffing subcommittees. The board, which should consist of 8 to 12 members regardless of the organization's size, should bring together people qualified to serve on the four most important committees: planning, compensation, auditing, and regulatory compliance. Detail-oriented financial executives should serve on the auditing committee. The compensation committee requires managers who are used to evaluating employees. And the planning committee needs creative visionaries.

The planning committee is key to answering the four questions. To ensure intellectual discipline, the planning process should be integrated with the budgeting process so that plans do not deteriorate into vague or extravagant statements of purpose. This subcommittee should include the most original thinkers on the board, those who are most likely to challenge the status quo. They are the people who can best articulate the organization's mission and determine whether its resources are fulfilling that mission.

Members of the compensation committee perform a particularly critical role as public scrutiny of salaries at nonprofits heightens. Although compensation committees usually perform their reviews by comparing the levels of compensation in their organization to those in other comparable nonprofit or business organizations, this process is not always sufficient. Clearly the public's opinion is that executives of nonprofit organizations

should *not* earn the same compensation as equivalent
business executives. The public has spoken with its
purse and reduced its charitable donations to nonprofits
whose executives earned
what they viewed as
excessive compensation.
While the public proba-
bly does not expect non-
profit executives to take
vows of poverty, it also
does not expect them to
receive lavish perks and earn salaries more than ten
times the average U.S. family income of $36,000 per year,
as many currently do.

*How comfortable would
compensation committee
members be if their names
appeared in a newspaper
story about nonprofit
executive salaries?*

Still, some board members believe that executives
should earn an amount equivalent to what they could
earn in the private sector. They argue strongly that nonprofits must compete for managerial talent on a level
playing field with for-profit organizations. But this argument is somewhat undercut by the fact that many professionals employed by nonprofits accept salaries lower
than they would receive in for-profit organizations. Ken-
neth Hodder, the national commander of the $1.3 billion
Salvation Army, widely admired for its managerial excellence, receives cash compensation of about $25,000 per
year.

Compensation committee members should evaluate
openly and honestly whether the organization's public
constituency may find the compensation of its executives excessive. They should avoid the practices of some
compensation committees, which engage in considerable subterfuge, hiding portions of their executives' compensation in bonuses and other perks or in unconsoli-
dated subsidiaries to avoid clear disclosure of the total

amount. Committee members should be prepared to explain publicly why they pay the salaries they do. A good way to check on their comfort with compensation levels is to ask how they would feel if their names appeared in a front-page story in the local newspaper about nonprofit executive compensation.

The auditing committee should supervise the organization's external and internal auditors, if they exist; oversee the preparation of its annual financial statements; and, most important, report the results to the other board members. Nonprofit accounting usually relies on fund accounting, a measurement system that greatly multiplies the complexities of the financial report. Because most board members are not familiar with this method of accounting, they may ignore the important information contained in the financial statements. An auditing committee's report that consists of a mind-numbing trip through these foreign-sounding statements is generally useless. Instead, the committee's presentation should explain how the financial statements answer the four questions discussed above. It should also include a review of the social and demographic characteristics of the organization's clients.

The regulatory compliance committee, which oversees the work of the organization's internal auditing staff and monitors the organization's adherence to the requirements of key government agencies, may prove helpful to heavily regulated nonprofits, heading off potentially serious problems. MIT, Harvard, and Stanford were among the research universities whose accounting for overhead expenses was challenged by the federal government. The expenses of Stanford University's yacht were allegedly among the inappropriate overhead expenses billed to the government. The challenges ultimately resulted in the return of substantial funds to the government and in considerable embarrassment to the institutions.

To prevent such problems, this committee would spell out the policies governing compliance and audit their implementation. At its best, it could inspire adherence to the spirit and not merely to the letter of the law. Outside compliance auditors, when they are used, should report to this committee.

To a limited extent, the members of these subcommittees should overlap, so that they are familiar with one another's work. But as overlapping membership increases, the ability of each committee to provide checks and balances on the others' work diminishes. If feasible, these committees should be supported by appropriate staff people, such as the top-level executives in the planning, financial, controllership, and human resource functions.

Nonprofit boards frequently ask too much or too little of their members. Some boards deluge their members with information about every event and hold weekly meetings, while others may send out a two-line agenda for an annual meeting that reads: "Item 1: Approval of Prior Meeting's Minutes. Item 2: New Business." Clearly neither approach is useful. Instead, board members should be asked to meet as frequently as necessary. The boards of small or entrepreneurial nonprofits should generally meet more frequently than those of larger, well-established ones. Organizations in crisis must meet more often than stable ones. A calendar of three to seven meetings a year is usually a good starting point.

OPEN COMMUNICATION IS CRUCIAL to making the four questions work. They will remain a theoretical exercise unless all board members understand them and are well versed in their measures. The board of directors of Bowdoin College in Brunswick, Maine, provides a good example of how to disseminate information effectively. All its members receive a thorough introductory grounding in their responsibilities on the board and in the measures associated with their work, as well as continuing education in issues relevant to the college. At each meeting, the chair of each subcommittee gives a full report, which is followed by an open debate. The voices of recent graduates are as welcome as those of more experienced board members, such as Leon Gorman, president of L.L. Bean.

Some Girl Scout councils take this process one step further, reporting results to the public as well. At a recent gathering of a Girl Scout council in Worcester, Massachusetts, administrators and board members hosted a public discussion about the organization's use of funds. One Girl Scout council had just been criticized on a national newsmagazine show, "Eye to Eye," which suggested that the council's staff members were hoarding most of the profits from cookie sales instead of using them to provide services for local troops. Rather than becoming defensive, the council discussed its revenue sources before an audience of nearly 200, consisting of Girl Scouts, volunteers, staff, and board members, and outlined how it used those funds to develop programs, maintain camps, and so on—the kind of full disclosure befitting an organization with an ethical agenda. Most important, the council solicited open debate on how best to use its resources. This kind of debate is critical to finding the best answers to the four questions—solutions that will allow board members to oversee productive organizations. Nonprofits form the backbone of the U.S. system for providing higher education, health care, and culture. And they represent the best hope for creating a more humane, literate society. But without effective oversight, nonprofits can easily lose sight of their mission, misusing funds or focusing on tangential issues. Only an informed and proactive board can ensure that an organization will fulfill its function, providing useful services for generations to come.

Note

1. Regina E. Herzlinger and William S. Krasker, "Who Profits from Nonprofits?" HBR, January–February 1987.

Originally published in July–August 1994
Reprint 94404

The author is grateful to Ramona Hilgenkamp, Jay Lorsch, Warren McFarlan, and the participants in the Seminar on Nonprofits at the Harvard Business School for their comments on this article, and to Diana Gaeta and Sarah Eriksen for their research assistance.

The New Work of the Nonprofit Board

BARBARA E. TAYLOR,

RICHARD P. CHAIT, AND

THOMAS P. HOLLAND

Executive Summary

TOO OFTEN, THE BOARD OF A NONPROFIT organization is little more than a collection of high-powered
people engaged in low-level activities. But that can
change, the authors say, if trustees are willing to discover
and take on the *new work* of the board. When they perform the new work, a board's members can significantly
advance the institution's mission and long-term welfare.

Doing the new work requires a board to engage in
new practices. First, the board must go beyond rubber-
stamping management's proposals and find out what
issues really matter to the institution. It can do that by
making the CEO paint the big picture of the organization's strategic concerns, by understanding key stakeholders, by consulting experts, and by deciding what
needs to be measured in order to judge the institution's
performance.

Second, a board doing the new work must take action: the board must not only set policy but also work with management to implement it. Third, the board must go beyond strictly functional organization: the new work requires flexibility and encourages ad hoc arrangements. Finally, board meetings—where boards underperform most visibly—should be driven by goals, not by processes.

The authors give many examples of boards that have successfully embraced the new work. The stakes are high: if boards demonstrate that they can change effectively, the professional staff at the institutions they serve just may follow suit.

EFFECTIVE GOVERNANCE by the board of a nonprofit organization is a rare and unnatural act. Only the most uncommon of nonprofit boards functions as it should by harnessing the collective efforts of accomplished individuals to advance the institution's mission and long-term welfare. A board's contribution is meant to be strategic, the joint product of talented people brought together to apply their knowledge and experience to the major challenges facing the institution.

What happens instead? Nonprofit boards are often little more than a collection of high-powered people engaged in low-level activities. Why? The reasons are myriad. Sometimes the board is stymied by a chief executive who fears a strong board and hoards information, seeking the board's approval at the last moment. Sometimes board members lack sufficient understanding of the work of the institution and avoid dealing with issues requiring specialized knowledge. Individual board members may not bring themselves fully to the task of governance, because board membership generally carries little personal accountability. And often the powerful individuals who make up the board are unpracticed in working as members of a team. No matter which cause predominates, nonprofit board members are often left feeling discouraged and underused, and the organization gains no benefit from their talents. The stakes remain low, the meetings process-driven, the outcomes ambiguous, and the deliberations insular. Many members doubt whether a board *can* have any real power or influence.

The key to improved performance is discovering and doing what we call the *new work* of the board. Trustees are interested in results. High-powered people lose energy when fed a steady diet of trivia. They may oblige management by discussing climate control for art exhibitions, the condition of old steam lines, or the design of a new logo, but they get charged up when searching for a new CEO, successfully completing a capital campaign, or developing and implementing a strategic plan. *New work* is another term for work that matters.

The new work has four basic characteristics. First, it concerns itself with crucial, do-or-die issues central to the institution's success. Second, it is driven by results that are linked to defined timetables. Third, it has clear measures of success. Finally, it requires the engagement of the organization's internal and external constituencies. The new work generates high levels of interest and demands broad participation and widespread support.

The New Work Requires New Practices

The new work defies the conventions that have regulated board behavior in the past. Whereas the customary work of a nonprofit board is limited to scrutinizing management, the new work requires new rules of engagement and unorthodox ways of fulfilling a board's responsibilities. The pressures on most nonprofits today are too great for the old model to suffice. Nonprofit leaders can take the following steps to improve board practices:

FIND OUT WHAT MATTERS

Traditionally, nonprofit boards and CEOs have agreed that management defines problems and recommends solutions. A board might refine management's proposals but rarely rejects any. Why? Few trustees know the industry or the institution well enough to do more, and those who do dread being labeled as meddlers or micromanagers. Board members sometimes are made to feel that asking a thorny question or advancing an alternative opinion is disloyal to the administration. A vote on an issue is a vote on the CEO. But how can a reactive, uninformed board know what opportunities the organization is missing? And how much damage must the organization sustain before the board realizes something is amiss?

To do the new work, trustees and management together must determine the important issues and the agenda of the organization. Trustees need to understand what the CEO sees as the critical issues. They also need to know what other stakeholders and industry experts think, because no chief executive knows enough to be a board's sole supplier of information and counsel. Knowledgeable trustees can help inform the CEO's judgment. They can also perform a useful function for the CEO by focusing the organization's attention on issues that are unpopular within it or that fall outside the staff's capabilities. In addition, the board can find out what matters by engaging in the following four sets of activities:

Make the CEO paint the big picture. The litmus test of the chief executive's leadership is not the ability to solve problems alone but the capacity to articulate key questions and guide a collaborative effort to formulate answers. As one member of a museum's board observes, "What I want most from the president are the big ideas." The CEO must be willing to share responsibility, and the board must be willing to follow the CEO's lead—and ask questions. "If you don't do that," says one college's trustee, "the board doesn't really have a clue about what is going on. When a problem arises and the CEO needs the trustees, they won't own the problem or be willing to help solve it."

The CEO should review the organization's foremost strategic challenges annually with the board. The board, for its part, must consider whether the CEO accurately targeted and defined the issues. This is a moment, maybe *the* moment, in which the board adds value. Together, the CEO and the board must agree on the institution's priorities and strategic direction. Those considerations, in turn, will shape the work of the board and its evaluation of the CEO.

The board of a college in the South has formalized this process successfully. At a retreat each January, the CEO and the trustees rank the most important challenges facing the institution. Then the board structures its committees to reflect those priorities. Last year, for example, the board concluded that marketing and technological infrastructure were its top concerns. The board formed task forces of trustees and constituents to study those issues, to specify the decisions the board would have to make during the coming year, and to clarify the board's needs for information and education. At the May board meeting, the task forces provided initial reports, and the board decided how to organize in order to pursue the issues. Trustees also developed measurable expectations for the president that were linked to the board's top concerns.

Get to know key stakeholders. Boards and CEOs have to know what matters to the constituents they serve. The interactions of the old work—which were mostly social events and show-and-tell sessions—will not do. The new work requires two-way communication. As a college president remarks, part of the reason for such communication is "to make the board vulnerable to constituents"—to make it accessible and accountable rather than insulated from the ordinary life of the institution. In that spirit, the boards of several colleges now meet routinely with leaders of student, faculty, and alumni bodies to explore matters of common concern.

The new work requires that board members and CEOs get to know their institutions' stakeholders.

Consider the example of a residential treatment center for children with emotional disabilities. When a major benefactor died, the center needed to find new sources of income. While interviewing leaders of social service organizations (a major source of referrals), several board members were shocked to discover that the center was seen as elitist and interested only in easy cases. In fact, many professionals referred the easy cases to less expensive care and assumed that the center would reject the difficult ones. Alarmed by these misperceptions, the trustees formed a task force to guide a public relations effort. The board expanded to include trustees with ties to sources of referrals and strengthened its relationships with other constituents through educational events and joint programming. "I want to make sure this board is never again so out of touch with its community," said the board's chair at the end of the process.

Close ties between the board and constituents unnerve CEOs who are determined to be the board's sole source of information and fear that direct communication between trustees and stakeholders will weaken time-honored lines of authority. That reaction puzzles board members; as one college trustee asks, "Why not have students talk to trustees? What's there to hide? These are our clients. I'm old enough and smart enough to know that some people just want to complain. Trustees are as qualified as the president to interpret the views they express. The closer I get to reality, the better I can sympathize with and help the CEO."

Consult experts. Many nonprofits are susceptible to competitive forces and to changes in public policy. Consider, for example, the impact on museums of cuts in funding by the National Endowment for the Arts, or the effect on hospitals of efforts to reform federally funded health care. Unless trustees understand the basic economics, demographics, and politics of the industry, boards will be hard pressed to separate the trivial from the significant and the good news from the bad. The new work requires learning about the industry from many sources.

One of those sources should be experts on the board itself. Although boards regularly recruit trustees with expertise in functional areas like finance, law, and mar-

Outside experts can help a board understand the effect of demographic changes on an institution.

keting, the new work requires a board to have more than a few trustees with relevant professional expertise: physicians on a hospital's board, academics on a college's board, social workers on a clinic's board. Expert trustees can guide fellow board members through a foreign culture. For example, one Ivy League institution counted a former university president among its board members. At one point, he criticized his colleagues for second-guessing the administration's disciplining of a fraternity, saying, "I'd be furious if my board did this." The board backed off. And at a liberal arts college, a trustee who was a professor at another school helped educate the board about the complexities of measuring teaching quality and reallocating academic positions from departments with declining enrollments to those with growing demand. At the same time, he helped establish the board's credibility with the faculty.

Another source of knowledge is outside experts. They can help boards understand competition, client demographics, trends in government support, and public policy debates. For example, the board of a Protestant theological seminary faced with declining enrollment conferred with experts on professional education, the economics of religious education, and the demographics of its own denomination. The trustees learned that their denomination's population would continue to decline, further eroding financial support for the seminary and job opportunities for new ministers. On its current course, the institution would be bankrupt in a few years. The seminary decided to leverage the strength of its high-quality faculty by becoming a resource to the broader Protestant community, offering theological education to laypeople and continuing education for church workers and ministers, both on campus and in local churches.

Decide what needs to be measured. Corporate boards typically monitor a limited number of performance indicators. Those vital signs convey the company's overall condition and signal potential problems. Nonprofit boards often lack comparable data, largely because the trustees and the staff have never determined what matters most.

Together, the board and management should identify 10 to 12 critical indicators of success. For a college, that may mean scrutinizing its tuition discount (the average remission the institution gives to students as financial aid). For a museum, it may mean measuring its total return on endowment investments. For a hospital, the board may monitor occupancy rates. Distinctive strategies can suggest novel measures. A boarding school focusing on computer literacy monitored the ratio between students' dial-ups to the campus network and their phone calls from their dorm rooms for pizza delivery. A rising percentage of network calls meant that students were becoming more comfortable with new technology. Using comparable creativity, an orchestra with an aging subscriber base monitored ticket sales to single people in their twenties and thirties who had attended chamber music programs with wine and cheese receptions held afterward.

Graphic comparisons against projections, past performance, or industry norms focus a board's attention on crucial issues and remind trustees that the ultimate goal of the board is to influence those indicators in a positive way. As the CEO of a college in the Midwest says, "We have a set of key performance indicators, explicitly linked to the strategic plan, that are reviewed at every meeting. We even put them on a pocket-size card that trustees can carry around."

ACT ON WHAT MATTERS

In the world of the old work, the lines were clearly drawn: the board remained on the policy-setting side of the net, management on the implementation side, and so the game of governance was played. In the new work, the board and management are on the same side of the net as partners in both roles.

In the new work, the board and management work together on both policy and implementation.

The question is not, Is this an issue of policy or implementation? Rather, the question is, Is the issue at hand important or unimportant, central or peripheral?

Today few nonprofits can risk barring the CEO from policy development or divorcing the board from policy implementation. In a capital campaign, establishing priorities and goals is setting policy, identifying prospects and making calls is implementation. In the search for a new CEO, determining selection criteria is

making policy, designing the procedure and conducting the interviews is implementation. In brief, most
important matters cannot be subdivided neatly into
policy or administration.

In many instances, implementation is far more consequential than formulation. (See "Focus on the Constellation, Not the Stars.") For example, in face-to-face meetings, trustees of a Catholic women's college persuaded
affluent older alumnae to support a new institutional
focus on serving poor minority women from the inner
city. The board of another college, troubled by the
decline in students able to pay full tuition, selected three
trustees to assist the administration with the design of a
marketing strategy aimed at attracting more students
able to pay.

In another case, a university owned a commercial
radio station. The board questioned how the station fit in
with the school's mission. After deciding with the president that the university
could turn profits from
the sale of the station to
better educational use,
the trustees negotiated
the transaction. Afterward, the president exulted, "This
was the board at its best." The board members knew
more than the staff about the radio business and about
selling a major asset, and they put that knowledge to use.

*For the new work to
happen, substance must
dictate a board's structure.*

Involving trustees in policy implementation can be
critically important during a crisis. In the aftermath of
the scandal at the United Way of America (the CEO
used more than a million dollars of United Way money
for personal expenses), the board and CEO of one local
chapter agreed that each of the trustees would interview

five business leaders to learn what the chapter might do to improve community support for an upcoming campaign. The advice was consistent: admit that the national organization had blundered badly, stop all payments to the national headquarters until the charges were resolved, promise that all funds would remain in the community, allow donor-designated contributions, and promise that the board would issue a public report on allocations. The CEO and the trustees accepted those recommendations and inaugurated an intense public-relations effort that engaged every board member. In the end, the campaign was almost as successful as the previous year's and was substantially more successful than those of other chapters in the region. That would not have been the case had the board only set policy.

ORGANIZE AROUND WHAT MATTERS

The board's new work must be organized to deal with the institution's priorities. That may seem self-evident, but boards often organize their work in functionally oriented committees (physical plant, finance, public relations) that channel trustees toward low-stakes operational decisions. For the new work to happen, substance must dictate structure. Committees, work groups, and task forces must mirror the institution's strategic priorities.

For instance, a theological seminary replaced most of its operationally oriented committees with ones that reflected the major goals of the strategic plan: globalizing the curriculum, improving relations with local churches, and providing continuing education for the ministry. The committees included trustees and constituents. One result: on the recommendation of the committee on church relations, the seminary established a clearinghouse to provide local churches with technical assistance in such areas as financial management, adult education, and church governance.

In another example, the board of a preeminent women's college has under active consideration the creation of four "councils" (business affairs, campus affairs, external affairs, and governance and board affairs) as umbrellas for clusters of standing committees. The council on campus affairs, for example, would oversee the activities and orchestrate the annual agendas of the student-life, admissions, and trustee-faculty relations committees, which would meet only as necessary. The council chairs would coordinate the annual agendas of the four councils and suggest strategic issues for in-depth discussion at board meetings.

Task forces that include constituents and nontrustee experts can tackle critical yet discrete matters such as outsourcing certain functions or installing a total quality management program. For example, the board of an independent day school appointed two task forces to explore accreditation issues with the appropriate state and federal agencies. The task forces gathered information about demographic trends, accreditation requirements, and possible legislation that would affect independent schools. At a special Saturday session, the task forces presented their findings, the board discussed whether to seek accreditation and whether to become more selective, *and* the task forces disbanded. The work had been done.

Such "tissue paper" task forces (use and discard) drive the board toward real-time results, multiply leadership opportunities, and prevent longtime members from dominating standing committees. As one college's trustee confesses, "Many of our standing committees don't really shape policy or identify needs. They're an empty ritual, a burden, not an asset. In contrast, task forces are very effective. For example, we're looking at the cost and shape of a marketing plan. A task force helped the board understand the problem and recommended directions. There was a material difference in the sense of ownership."

FOCUS MEETINGS ON WHAT MATTERS

Boards are boards only in meetings, and yet meetings are where boards underperform most visibly. Many trustees think that lack of time is the most significant barrier to a board's ability to perform the new work. In fact, the greater problem is the failure to determine what matters and to let that imperative drive the frequency, format, and duration of board and committee meetings. And if a board can meet only infrequently or for short periods, trustees should consider realistically what they can deliver. The chair, the CEO, and perhaps the executive committee should design each meeting by asking the questions, What is the purpose of this meeting? and How can we organize it to fulfill that purpose? Four common responses will help illustrate the point.

We need more background to make a decision.
This answer calls for a discussion led by a moderator. Discussion sessions can engage and educate the entire board about issues facing the institution. The goal is to air views, invite questions, and consider alternatives— not to win an argument. No specific decision is on the table, and no votes are taken.

Consider the case of the college board that was generally concerned—but not sufficiently informed—about the interrelated issues of student quality, tuition charges, and financial aid. Each year, the finance committee, usually under pressure to balance the next year's budget, presented a tuition recommendation to the board. The process afforded no practical opportunity for the board to study the causes and effects of tuition increases. Last year, the board convened explicitly to learn more about the effect of tuition and financial aid decisions on enrollment and student quality, as well as on the bottom line. Subsequently, the board devised principles to govern the finance committee's recommendations for the following year. Those principles included the decision to hold institutionally funded financial aid to below 25% of overall tuition but to use grants to attract better students. The board also decided to increase average class size in order to free up resources to enhance learning partnerships, including student-faculty research projects.

At another university, each of the board's key committees appears once a year before the whole board for a half-day session to present information on a substantive issue or special area. For example, the finance committee led a board session to explain capital budgeting, deferred maintenance, and depreciation of assets. A task force on instructional technology that included faculty and students held a panel discussion to describe the state of the art across the nation and how technology was being used on their campus to transform the learning process. As a result of such sessions, reports the chair, "The whole board becomes more knowledgeable about the issues. The old bean counters on the finance committee now see other aspects of the institution."

We don't know what to do about a current problem. The new work, by definition, grapples with complicated issues that defy easy solutions. Trustees and management must be able to present multiple perspectives and develop solutions that reflect the group's best thinking. A meeting's design is critical to making that happen. Discussion must center on the explicit question at hand, such as, What should be our top three priorities for the capital campaign? or What specific steps can the board take to improve ties to the corporate community?

Small groups create a more comfortable environment for trustees to speak freely. Says one college board member, "I may have a comment worthy of 16 ears, but not one worthy of 60." Small groups provide venues for brainstorming, arenas where there are no dumb questions or insane ideas. A board member of a midwestern university explains, "Before we added small group discussions, all 50 trustees sat passively and listened to a few people impart information. The process was superficial, and substantive participation was limited to the executive committee. Small groups allow everyone to participate genuinely."

We face a crisis. In times of crisis, business-as-usual must be pushed aside to allow the board to concentrate on the matter at hand. Crises might include the loss of a major source of funding, the sudden departure or death of the CEO, the rise of a competitor, or even a split within the board itself.

For example, a local Alzheimer's Association chapter lost a major grant in 1993 and had no immediate prospects for significant new funding. The chair called a special meeting of the board to discuss restructuring the chapter's services. A review of the mission statement reminded trustees of the organization's purpose; an examination of what it would mean to reengineer the organization helped open up discussion of key issues. By the end of the meeting, board members accepted responsibility for specific tasks to help manage the crisis: explaining the chapter's mission to potential sponsors in the community, exploring the restructuring experiences of other chapters, and examining with staff the best ways to smooth the transition to a smaller, more tightly focused organization.

We need to deal with sensitive governance issues. Executive sessions without the CEO present open lines of communication among trustees. "We have an executive session after each board meeting," says one college trustee. "We feel free to bring up anything at all. This is a time for us to really ask questions and probe." Among the questions a board might entertain in an executive session are, Did we deal with important issues? How did the meeting go? Can we better serve the CEO? Differences of opinion among trustees or between the board and the CEO can be treated more candidly in an executive session. Says one board member of a women's college in the South, "If there are sensitive issues, the executive session gives us a chance to counsel one another."

These examples of the new work and new structures are far from exhaustive. Boards should experiment with different formats for different purposes. Use what works. (See "Teaching an Old Board New Work," page 71.)

Leading the Way

Trustees protest regularly that artists, academics, physicians, and other professionals stubbornly resist change. Yet governing boards are among the least innovative, least flexible elements of many nonprofits. Boards are as reluctant to forsake committees as faculty members and physicians are to eliminate departments. Trustees resist varied formats for board meetings more than musicians resist novel formats for concerts. And board members oppose new membership criteria as strongly as teachers oppose nontraditional certification.

This hypocrisy was plain to the chair of a midwestern university's board. "It's tough for a group like this to be self-conscious. They're classic CEOs. They can tell stories about empowerment and team building, but that's not how they got where they are. They are uncomfortable with questions like How are we doing? and How should we improve? Most of our members are heavy into productivity. The board isn't hesitant to ask faculty and administrators to answer these questions. The board wants everyone else's time to be more efficient and effective, but the board should look for ways to improve, too."

Too often, trustees assume that organizational success proves that the board has performed well, even when there is little evidence that the board played a significant role, and even when staff members say privately that the success was achieved *despite* the board. "Most boards have the attitude," a trustee of a women's college notes, "that if it ain't broke, don't fix it, but I think it's better to fix it before it breaks." A sympathetic explanation for the reluctance of most boards to experiment with substantial governance reforms would be the trustees' desire to do no harm. A less charitable explanation would be the trustees' desire to do no work.

Moving to the new work takes work. As the CEO of a midwestern university recounted after the institution's board had changed, "It required getting people out of their little corners, the areas that they had learned and owned. They wanted to work on what they knew best and leave the rest to others. They had to rotate around and learn everything in order to govern the organization. They've moved from being just guardians of the physical plant, overseers of the administration, and suits with deep pockets."

Boards across the nonprofit sector are calling on institutions to change. As trustees demand evidence of productivity gains, efficient processes, and enhanced outcomes, they should model the behavior they seek in others. If boards demonstrate the capacity to discard shibboleths, dismantle old structures, and desert deeply ingrained modes of operation, the professional staff may follow suit. If the board does not do the new work, the trustees' hypocrisy will be blatant, and the value added by the board will be too meager to inspire organizational reform.

Teaching an Old Board New Work

Old Work

1. Management defines problems, assesses options, and proposes solutions. Board listens, learns, approves, and monitors.

2. Board sets policy, which management implements. Respective territories are sharply defined; there is little or no border traffic. Domains are decided by organization chart.

3. Structure of standing committees parallels administrative functions. Premium is on permanent structure, established

routines. Members occupy functional niches. Board maintains busywork.

4. Board meetings are process driven. Protocol doesn't vary. Function follows form. Emphasis is on transmission of information and reports.

5. Board is a collection of stars. It recruits people with an eye to expertise and status. The CEO cultivates individual relationships and exploits each trustee's talents.

New Work

1. Board and management discover issues that matter, mutually determine the agenda, and solve problems together.

2. Board and management both set policy and implement it. Lines are blurred, borders open. Domains are decided by nature of issue at hand.

3. Structure of board mirrors institution's strategic priorities. Premium is on flexibility, ad hoc arrangements. Members occupy functional intersections. Board creates centers of action.

4. Board meetings are goal driven. Protocol varies with circumstances. Form follows function. Emphasis is on participation and action.

5. Board is a constellation. It recruits team members with an eye to personality and overall chemistry. Board cultivates group norms and collective capabilities of trustees.

Focus on the Constellation, Not the Stars

HISTORICALLY, the practice of most large, well-established nonprofits has been to recruit stars as board members.

The assumption was that a collection of exceptional individuals would equal an exceptional board. The new work of the board cannot be done by a powerful inner circle. Instead, everyone must get involved. That will set off a chain reaction: the more trustees are involved in meaningful work, the more they will know; the more they know, the more they can contribute to the team; and the more they contribute to the team, the more likely the stars will form a constellation.

Too often, an executive committee makes all the important decisions and expects the rest of the board to comply. As one university trustee reports, "The executive committee is a little closed club of trustees who give lip service to inclusiveness but don't really practice it. It's nice, I know, to have all that control, but it's not good for the rest of the board." In those situations, trustees outside the loop of power lose interest.

To function as a team, board members need equal and timely access to information. Agendas, minutes, and background information from task force and committee meetings should be distributed to all trustees, and the board should use technology—conference calls and E-mail—to increase timely communication. Executive-committee meetings should be open to all members of the board, and board and committee chairs should be coached to invite reticent trustees to speak, as well as to avoid premature closure of debates.

Given the collaborative character of the new work, prospective trustees should understand that governance is a collective enterprise. They should realize that the board will expect more than attendance, participation, and financial support. The holy trinity of wealth, work, and wisdom (sometimes in just that order!) that has guided the selection of trustees in the past must be changed. Says one trustee of a college in the Midwest, "The operating principle for selection was to add as many friends as you could, in the hope that some of them would turn out to be helpful. That's a poor approach."

A better approach is to engage potential trustees as members of a task force or a committee so that everyone can become better acquainted—a mutual tryout. Rather than extend an invitation to join the board based chiefly on a prospect's track record, arrange a conversation to explore the fit between the individual and the institution and its board. Some entrepreneurs, industrial captains, and self-employed professionals, for instance, are intolerant of the convoluted decision-making processes and dispersed powers characteristic of most nonprofits. Those individuals, however successful, are unlikely to be effective trustees. Board members should love the organization for what it is as well as for what they hope to make it.

The capacity for team play will be enhanced if new trustees are incorporated as swiftly as possible into the new work of the board. New recruits need to know of recent strategic decisions and current challenges. In addition, the board might accommodate the committee preferences of new trustees so that the rookies can play comfortable positions and thus gain self-confidence and respect from their peers.

A mentoring program that matches a seasoned trustee with a new trustee provides another way to foster fellowship and to engage newcomers faster. On one board, the pair are seated together for the first year so that the mentor can quietly explain the history of issues before the board, answer questions, decipher the board's unwritten rules, and debrief the new trustee after meetings. A more careful approach to the selection of trustees, combined with a mentoring program, can help a board form the constellation it needs to work at peak effectiveness.

Originally published in September–October 1996
Reprint 96509

When a Business Leader Joins a Nonprofit Board

WILLIAM G. BOWEN

Executive Summary

DO WELL-REGARDED REPRESENTATIVES OF THE BUSI-
NESS WORLD often check their toughness at the door of
the nonprofit boardroom? A number of widely publicized cases suggest that the answer is yes, and many
business executives agree. What is the explanation?

In this adaptation from his most recent book, William
Bowen, president of the Andrew W. Mellon Foundation
and the former president of Princeton University, argues
that nonprofit boards have much to learn from the business world. But a combination of inappropriate motivations and unfamiliar and uncomfortable situations can
prevent businesspeople from contributing effectively in a
nonprofit setting. People from the for-profit world often
join a nonprofit board to take a vacation from the bottom line and to shed their "barbarian" image. They may

therefore be less disciplined than nonprofit organizations need them to be.

For many people from the for-profit sector, joining a nonprofit board involves venturing into unknown territory. Board members with no visceral feel for an organization may bring inappropriate values to the table. And individuals familiar with corporate financial accounts may find it difficult to penetrate the intricacies of fund accounting. If the management and staff of a nonprofit organization are hostile to board members with business backgrounds, these directors will find their jobs even more difficult. In turn, corporate representatives may feel intimidated by or contemptuous of nonprofit professionals.

The management and staff of nonprofit organizations can help facilitate more effective participation by business executives, but businesspeople themselves must make a considerable effort to contribute their skills, discipline, and know-how in this unfamiliar realm.

Is IT TRUE THAT WELL-REGARDED REPRESENTATIVES of the business world are often surprisingly ineffective as members of nonprofit boards? Do they somehow seem to have checked their analytical skills and their "toughness" at the door? If this is true in some considerable number of cases, what is the explanation? And what, if anything, can be done about it?

These questions are consequential precisely because it is so important that highly qualified individuals from "the world of affairs" serve on nonprofit boards—and serve effectively. They are needed for their knowledge, skills, and general competence. They are also needed for fund-raising, for contacts, and, in part, for the sake of appearances. It is hard to identify a major nonprofit board that lacks business representation. I cannot think of any.

Although it would be difficult to devise a rigorous empirical test, I suspect that my harsh-sounding proposition questioning the effectiveness of nonprofit board members from the business sector holds with surprising frequency. This impression is certainly widely shared— by many business executives, among others. There have also been some well-publicized examples. The business representatives on the United Way board, for example, certainly appear to have failed to do a proper job of overseeing the activities of that organization. At Morris Brown College in Atlanta, Georgia, observers have linked the college's severe financial problems with the board's inability to ask the right questions. Of Morris Brown's 30 trustees, 15 were business professionals. And press accounts of the Empire Blue Cross debacle have regularly referred to the lack of proper oversight on the part of outside directors, who were a mix of health care professionals and individuals with business backgrounds. According to the accounts, board scrutiny did not adhere to the basic standards of the corporate world.

Needless to say, there are also many instances in which my proposition does not hold. Hanna Gray, former president of the University of Chicago, says that in her experience "[business] CEOs tend to be the *best* board members; they are more likely than others to understand how complex organizations function." My experience confirms this observation. At both Princeton University and the Mellon Foundation, trustees with extensive experience in the business world have been highly effective. In short, the range of performance by business executives is very wide indeed, extending from extremely disappointing to outstanding. But whatever the exact number of disappointing experiences, we have here a phenomenon in search of an explanation.

Why Join a Nonprofit Board?

Fortunately, many busy executives join nonprofit boards because of deep personal commitments to the organizations' values and purposes. But others, I suspect, participate for reasons of status and with the expectation that they will be able to enjoy a kind of vacation from the bottom line. At least part of the motivation for joining a nonprofit board may be the enjoyment of membership in a new "club" (albeit one with potentially high dues when the time comes for trustees to make campaign contributions) that will provide a respite from morning-to-night struggles with earnings and balance sheets. The pleasure derived from such an association would be marred by the burden of having to say no to obviously meritorious requests for budgetary support. I was told, for example, that the board of one private secondary school with severe financial difficulties nonetheless approved a request from a group of teachers for new equipment because "they just couldn't say no to such dedicated teachers."

Business executives can't soften their "barbarian" image by playing the part of the bad cop.

Some executives join nonprofit boards in part to shed the "barbarian" image that may otherwise afflict them— either in their own perceptions or in the perceptions of others. If one's objective is to soften that image, it will not do to play the part of the bad cop by insisting that the organization retrench, that it can't afford salary increases for abominably paid staff members, and so on. Providing vocal support for impassioned statements of needs, even when that might seem imprudent, can be a nonbarbarian way of behaving. But such behavior may signal a board member's reluctance to blow the proverbial whistle on extravagant, overly optimistic, or even poorly conceived proposals.

The former director of a small arts organization has described a situation in which such permissiveness hindered a board's performance. She was earning a low salary as director of the organization, whereas her board members were, for the most part, wealthy individuals from the business world. Some board members evidently felt guilty about the director's low salary, and every summer they asked her why she didn't just take the summer off. She would reply that there was a lot of work

Board members with no visceral feel for an organization may bring values to the table that are simply inappropriate.

to be done, and that if board members wanted to help, they could raise more money so that the organization could hire more support staff. Instead, the board members attempted to assuage their sense of inequity by allowing the hardworking, low-paid director certain privileges that were not in the organization's best interest. Someone had to mind the store, as the trustees should have understood.

The consequences of too much permissiveness can be extremely serious, in part because other trustees may well defer to seasoned executives when it comes to business matters. As one trustee from the academic world confessed, "I just assumed that if there were a serious financial problem, surely [Jones and Smith], with all of their corporate experience, would tell us." Unfortunately, Jones and Smith did not speak up, and the organization in question nearly failed and may still fail. In retrospect, the board member from academia made a bad mistake in deferring to his business colleagues rather than trusting his own judgment about the seriousness of the financial difficulties confronting the institution.

Other motivations for joining boards represent a more general set of problems for certain classes of nonprofits. For example, the commendable desire of many college and university graduates to "give something back" can lead them to inject excessive doses of nostalgia into boardroom deliberations—what colleagues at Princeton used to call the furry-tiger syndrome.

Nonprofits of all kinds suffer from the presence of board members out to advance personal agendas. The former president of a foundation posed this question:

> *What is it that tends to rush in to fill the vacuum left in nonprofits by the absence of a bottom line? My experience . . . left me jaundiced about this, for it seemed to me that human vanity and a desire to be kept excited about the wonders of the foundation were what rushed in. Too often, trustees wanted to be able to brag about what [the foundation] was doing.*

While personal agendas can be a problem on corporate boards too, the need to focus on business outcomes is at least somewhat constraining.

Barriers to Success

For some people from the for-profit sector, joining a nonprofit board involves venturing into unknown territory. The boards of nonprofit organizations may include individuals who, while highly competent in some general sense, fail to understand how a ballet company functions or how graduate education relates to undergraduate education. Board members with no visceral feel for an organization may bring values to the board table that are simply inappropriate. I have heard of a

Accounting "experts" may be embarrassed to admit that they don't understand the intricacies of nonprofit financial statements.

case in which a businessman on the board of a church kept pushing for "double-digit growth" no matter what the implications were for the church's capacity to fulfill its mission.

An even more pervasive source of difficulty is that individuals familiar with corporate financial accounts may find it difficult to penetrate the intricacies of fund accounting. They are certainly far from alone in this respect, but because they are presumed to be experts in such matters, they may be especially embarrassed to acknowledge that they don't quite understand the financial statements of the nonprofit organization.

Board members' reluctance to come to grips with financial difficulties may have another source: concluding that an organization faces severe financial difficulties has implications for the trustees, often including the need to raise appreciably more money. If a board member does not want to participate actively in an aggressive fund-raising effort, the individual may be reluctant to emphasize the danger signals revealed by the organization's financial statements. Arjay Miller, former dean of Stanford Business School and former president of Ford, has suggested a golfing analogy: if a member of a golf club complains about the greens, he or she could end up

chairing the greens committee. A link between the failure to perceive signs of financial distress and a lack of
enthusiasm for new fund-raising tasks can be largely
unconscious, but I suspect it is real, in at least some
instances. It may just be more comfortable for some
trustees to draw down endowment, hope for a brighter
day, and allow events to unfold.

Given that courts are reluctant to hold volunteers to
a high standard of accountability, serving on a nonprofit
board may seem risk-free. On almost all nonprofit
boards, trustees can simply walk away if conditions
become adverse. That may not be true if certain kinds of
debt have been taken on and creditors are at the door,
but even then assets are usually more than sufficient to
cover obligations.

The fact that individual trustees are rarely identified
with troubled nonprofits, even in highly publicized situations, also makes it easier for them to disengage. Press
accounts usually refer to boards as corporate bodies,
sometimes naming the chairperson but rarely any other
members. Perhaps, as some have suggested, associating
individual trustees more
directly with the organi-
zations they serve would
increase accountability;
but I'm not sure how
much difference that
would really make. After
all, one's professional reputation as an investment
banker, for example, is not likely to be harmed by having
served on the board of a struggling nonprofit organization—particularly if one is perceived as having labored
hard to save it. In contrast, prominent board members
of a failed business undertaking can bear scars indefi-

*Serving on a nonprofit
board is usually risk-free,
but prominent trustees
of a failed business
can bear scars indefinitely.*

nitely. With less at stake, trustees of nonprofits may not look as closely at the numbers or pursue complex issues as doggedly as they would in a for-profit setting.

A very different explanation for what may seem like board members' incompetence or indifference, when neither is the case, has to do with the nature of the missions served by many nonprofit organizations. Robert Kasdin, treasurer and chief investment officer of the Metropolitan Museum of Art, attributes many of the difficulties encountered by business trustees to their being asked to play roles that, in his words, "raise unfamiliar types of normative questions."

To what extent, for example, is a museum justified in exceeding an endowment spending limit in order to invest in a new conservation facility, library, or gallery? Informed decisions in such situations require a rather sophisticated understanding of the implications of *not* spending money, as well as of spending it, and a willingness to make hard intergenerational choices: What will be the long-term effects of either decision on the quality of the institution and on its value to scholars in the future? How do the present and future benefits that can be gained through investments of this kind compare with the need to protect the core finances of the institution into the next generation by preserving the real value of the endowment? For-profit corporations also make present-versus-future choices all the time, but at least they have quantitative methodologies to guide them in framing the issues and projecting rates of return.

Staff Attitudes and Subtle Intimidation

If it is intrinsically difficult for an outsider to address questions that depend on a nuanced understanding of the mission of the institution and the choices before it, it is even harder to do so if the management and staff are unhelpful. A potential problem in some nonprofit organizations is that the professional staff may be so conscious of the unique qualities of their institution, and so sensitive to their obligation to be the guardians of its uniqueness, that, perhaps unknowingly, they will patronize or even dismiss the "unwashed" business executive. As Jed Bergman, my colleague at the Mellon Foundation, put it: "After all, this is *their* field; they are the ones who have studied the arts, or medicine, or science. And the more dire the circumstances, the more likely it is that members of the staff will feel a compulsion to 'save' the institution—even from the trustees."

The driving force is often not institutional loyalty alone. Many of the key employees of a nonprofit organization are professionals who may well feel as much loyalty to their profession, and to the norms inculcated in them when they were trained, as they do to any particular employer. The consequence may be a determination to hold a particular employer to what are considered universal standards (regarding de-accessioning, for example, in the museum world), regardless of local conditions. Lay trustees, especially those from the business world, may be considered, fairly or unfairly, insensitive to, if not ignorant of, these professional norms.

A related problem stems from the tendency of some individuals who have chosen to work in the nonprofit sector to harbor a thinly veiled hostility toward professionals from the profit-making sector. If business leaders fear being perceived as ax-wielding barbarians, that fear may not be entirely unfounded. And such perceptions can lead staff members to phrase questions and present information to board members in such a way that there appears to be one "right" answer. This protective attitude may not be challenged within the cloister of a nonprofit organization as rigorously as it might be in a for-profit enterprise. Louis Gerstner, chairman and CEO of IBM and a member of various nonprofit boards, suggests that staff members in nonprofits are sometimes defensive and unresponsive because they are less used to constructive criticism than are staff members in corporations, which are more likely, he suggests, to have accepted a "culture of challenge."

But an odd kind of subtle (or not so subtle) intimidation can work in the opposite direction. High-achieving corporate representatives do not want to seem ill informed, narrowly educated, or boorish by apparently failing to understand the reasons for an action that the nonprofit "pros" insist is essential. As Alice Emerson, former president of Wheaton College, recalls, some business executives on the board of the college still thought of the faculty as their teachers and thus were reluctant to argue with them.

Needless to say, by no means all board members, whatever their backgrounds, are so reverent. In fact, some have been known to display more than a little contempt for "impractical intellectuals." The healthiest relationships, at least in my experience, exist between board members and staff members who genuinely respect one another. This kind of relationship is obviously easier if the board member from the business world has some real understanding of the fields served by the nonprofit organization.

Frederick Borsch, Episcopal bishop of Los Angeles, who has served on and worked with the boards of many community service organizations, has emphasized the need for trustees to understand the laborious and time-consuming decision-making processes that often characterize these nonprofit organizations. "Some businesspeople are poor board members of nonprofits because they can't stand the slower, more collegial pace of decision making," he says. "They want everything settled *now*."

T HE POINT OF THESE COMMENTS is not to criticize members of nonprofit boards who come to their posts from successful careers in business; such people are badly needed. My intention is to warn unsuspecting leaders of nonprofit organizations, other board members, and staff members not to assume that directors with business qualifications will necessarily contribute the same hard-nosed approach in this setting that they are known to exhibit in their professional lives.

But we do not need to throw up our hands in despair. There are positive actions that the management and staff of nonprofit organizations can take to help facilitate more effective participation by business executives in discussions of priorities, resource allocation, and financial planning. There should be a conscious effort to make board reviews and board deliberations as trustee-friendly as possible. Moreover, board members with business experience should be encouraged to be as disciplined, or even more disciplined, in assessing the condition of a nonprofit organization as they would be in a profit-making setting. "Tough love" is needed here every bit as much as it is in the for-profit world, but people in nonprofit organizations often ignore that imperative.

Nonprofit boards have much to learn from certain disciplines characteristic of corporate boards—especially the routine use of benchmark data and the constant monitoring of discrepancies between results and planned outcomes. Experienced business executives can contribute to nonprofit organizations by insisting that commendable motives and high hopes are not enough.

For these reasons and others, it is critically important that the ablest people in the business world make the considerable effort necessary to function effectively in what may seem to be a strange realm—one in which missions are sometimes difficult to define with precision, resources are almost always scarce, and relevant data and analyses are either unavailable or slippery to the touch. But moving successfully from one realm to the other is far from easy, and everyone would be helped by fuller and franker recognition of the difficulties involved in transforming good intentions into effective board leadership.

Originally published in September–October 1994
Reprint 94504

Virtuous Capital

What Foundations Can Learn from Venture Capitalists

CHRISTINE W. LETTS,

WILLIAM RYAN, AND

ALLEN GROSSMAN

Executive Summary

U.S. FOUNDATIONS AND NONPROFITS work diligently on behalf of society's most needy and yet report that progress is slow and social problems persist. How can they learn to be more effective with their limited resources?

Foundations should consider expanding their mission from investing only in program innovation to investing in the organizational needs of nonprofit organizations as well. Their overemphasis on program design has meant deteriorating organizational capacity at many nonprofits.

If foundations are to help nonprofits be assured of making payroll, paying the rent, or buying a much-needed computer, they must develop hands-on partnering skills. Venture capital firms offer a helpful benchmark. In addition to putting up capital, they closely monitor the companies in which they have invested, provide

92   *Letts, Ryan, and Grossman*

management support, and stay involved long enough to see the company become strong. If foundation officers familiarize themselves with such practices, they can begin to build organizational capacity in the nonprofit sector.

Foundations can hire organizational experts to assist grantees; they can lengthen grant terms to allow non-profits to build up organizational strengths; and they can create new classes of grants that allow for organiza-tional effectiveness. Nonprofits in turn should articulate their organizational needs when applying for grants; they should apply to foundations known for longer-term grants; and they should create plans that justify long-term support from foundations.

FOR DECADES, foundations have been making large grants to nonprofit organizations in the hope of meet-ing a wide range of society's most pressing and vital needs. In 1995 alone, foundations invested more than $10 billion in programs dealing with, for example, poverty, homelessness, the environment, education, and the arts. Even as these large sums of money are put to work, however, many people in the nonprofit field are reporting a growing frustration that their pro-grams' goals, although valuable and praiseworthy, are not being achieved. Many social programs begin with high hopes and great promise, only to end up with lim-ited impact and uncertain prospects.

Forces beyond the control of either foundations or nonprofit organizations account for some of the prob-lems. For one thing, the federal government has scaled back funding for social services, leaving the foundations and nonprofits without an ally they had come to rely on. Furthermore, many leaders of nonprofits are finding that, despite their best efforts, social problems persist and may even be worsening. But part of the difficulty needs to be traced back to the relationship between the foundations and the nonprofits.

Traditionally, foundations make grants based on their assessment of the potential efficacy of a program. Although that approach creates an incentive for nonprofits to devise innovative programs, it does not encourage them to spend time assessing the strengths, goals, and needs of their own organizations. Thus they often lack the organizational resources to carry out the programs they have so carefully designed and tested. Foundations need to find new ways to make grants that not only fund programs but also build up the organizational capabilities that nonprofit groups need for delivering and sustaining quality.

Many foundations are well aware of the problem and are trying new approaches. In particular, some foundations have been studying venture capital firms and their techniques for guiding their portfolio companies through the early stages of organizational development. The idea makes sense. Clearly, foundations and venture capitalists face similar challenges: selecting the most worthy recipients of funding, relying on young organizations to implement ideas, and being accountable to the third party whose funds they are investing.

To gain a better understanding of just which venture capital practices could be put to use in the nonprofit sector, we brought together a number of leaders of foundations, nonprofit groups, and venture capital firms. Their insights helped clarify for us what foundations can learn from venture capitalists. As Edward Skloot, executive director of New York's Surdna Foundation, puts it, a closer study of venture capital practices can inspire foundations "to make a new set of rules to play by."

The State of Foundation Funding

In the words of former Ford Foundation president Franklin Thomas, philanthropy has seen itself as "the research and development arm of society." In the 1960s, for example, there was a tacit division of labor between foundations and the public sector. Foundations focused on research and develop-

Nonprofit programs begun with high hopes often end up with limited impact.

ment. If new ideas proved successful, the federal government would embrace them and assume responsibility for their widespread implementation through government agencies. Several of the signature programs of President Lyndon B. Johnson's War on Poverty, for example, were developed and tested in demonstrations funded by foundations.

To carry out their R&D role, foundations organize around program development. Grants are given primarily to develop and test new ideas. The grant funds the program demonstration, the evaluation of the early results, and, occasionally, the promotion of the findings to create interest in the program elsewhere. Although this R&D approach has been quite successful in stimulating innovative program ideas, it is clearly not suited to building the organizational strength necessary for the widespread and sustained implementation of those ideas. In the process of making a grant, foundations often overlook the organizational issues that could make or break the nonprofit. Instead, they fold organizational requirements into the category of routine overhead costs—costs that divert precious resources from the real work of delivering programs. Foundations' attitudes have long encouraged nonprofit organizations to focus on mission and to regard organizational capacity as worthwhile in principle but a distracting burden in practice. Hence a serious problem for the nonprofit sector: no one is investing in nonprofit organizational capacity.

The lack of support has meant that a number of specific needs at the nonprofits are routinely underfunded. The urgent and neglected requisites of organization building include funds to track the needs of the nonprofits' clients and how those needs are changing; time for nonprofit staff to plan new programs and processes; training and development for managers; and sound operating systems in the areas of finance, quality, and human resource development. Until those needs are addressed, the impact of programs will be limited.

Identifying Relevant Venture-Capital Practices

It is helpful to compare some of the differences in how venture capitalists interact with their start-up companies and how foundations work with nonprofit organizations. These differences can be the starting point for a process of reflection and change in the nonprofit sector.

RISK MANAGEMENT

Perhaps the most striking difference between venture capital firms and foundations is in how they manage risk. Many venture-capital investors believe that out of a portfolio of ten investments, only two will be "moon rockets"—ventures that produce a big payoff with a successful initial public offering. The rest may be projects that have a chance of going public someday, projects that will survive but probably won't issue stock, or projects that will fail outright. If a firm has too many project failures, future investors may be scared off and the venture capital fund itself may fail. It is in response to those risks that venture capital firms have developed many of their organization-building skills.

Foundations generally face little risk when making grants. Far from worrying about losing money, foundations are more likely to worry about not spending *enough*. (Failing to meet the IRS mandate that they pay out 5% of their assets annually means steep financial sanctions.) Because their funds are not at risk, foundations have not had to implement the kinds of controls that venture capitalists use. They rarely tie the compensation and career prospects of their program officers to the performance of grantees. Hence the program officers feel little pressure to learn and apply organizational lessons on the next round of grants. Unlike a venture capital firm, a foundation can prosper—and even bask in the glow of good works—with little risk of being tarnished by the weak performance of grantees.

PERFORMANCE MEASURES

The venture capital firm and the start-up begin building their relationship around financial and organizational projections, which then act as a set of performance measures. The measures, which can include cash flow, sales, profits, or market share, are continually updated to reflect the start-up company's progress and the market conditions. Clear objectives give the investors and the start-up managers a focus for their working relationship.

Like venture capitalists and start-ups, foundations and nonprofits share a goal: theirs is to improve conditions in the social sectors in which they operate.

Foundations focus on program efficacy; the long-term strength of their grantees takes the back seat.

Although it can be difficult to quantify such goals—for example, when the program is targeting inner-city development—the foundation and the nonprofit usually agree that the problem needs attention. However, foundations do *not* share one important goal of nonprofits. The nonprofit has a very explicit need to keep its organization healthy in terms of staff, revenue, and basic operating systems; the foundation, with its focus on program efficacy and its practice of making one-, two-, or three-year grants, does little to support those long-term goals. The sad irony is that although the nonprofit may serve its clients well in the short term, it may end up lacking the organizational strength it needs to continue its work.

CLOSENESS OF THE RELATIONSHIP

To enhance the prospects for growth and sustainability, the venture capitalist offers a range of noncash, value-added assistance. For example, investors will often take one or more seats on the company's board to help shape strategy. To supplement formal governance, the venture firm's officers engage in extensive coaching and mentoring of the start-up's senior managers. Furthermore, the venture capitalist gets involved in critical hiring decisions, such as the succession that takes place when some of the early founders are replaced with professional managers. The quality of the venture capitalist's input can be critical to success: *whose* money the start-up gets can be as important as how *much* the company gets or how much it pays for that money.

The bulk of a foundation's work comes even before a grant is made—in screening applications or seeking out new ideas. Once a grant has been made, the foundation assumes an *oversight* role to uncover poor management rather than a *partnering* role to develop capable management and adaptive strategies. Many program officers are reluctant to get involved with their grantees' organizational problems. For example, foundations require periodic financial reports but are unlikely to contribute the services of an expert to work with the nonprofit on financial planning. Most foundations never take a seat on a nonprofit board or act as mentors or partners: in fact, they believe that such involvement would be intrusive.

Foundations assume an oversight role instead of a partnering role that would develop strong managers.

Even foundations that do commit to the capacity building of nonprofit organizations often do so at arm's length. They hire third-party consultants who work on the nonprofit's particular organizational needs, such as back-office systems or professional development. However, because of the foundation's sensitivity about interference, the third-party consultant usually reports back only to the nonprofit. Hence the foundation loses the opportunity to learn about organizational needs or to respond effectively to them in the future. To be fair, the arm's-length relationship between a foundation and a nonprofit is partly due to the large workloads carried by foundation officers. The typical foundation officer handles hundreds of grant requests and scores of actual grants each year, as opposed to the venture capitalist officer, who manages maybe five or six companies at a time. Clearly, this oversize load of grants is something that foundations need to attend to if good organization building is going to take place.

AMOUNT OF FUNDING

As an industry, venture capitalist firms fund a very small percentage of the businesses that are started each year, but the impact that venture capitalists have on their start-up companies is quite significant. That is because the venture firm, once it has made the commitment, can help the start-up get the funding it needs to grow. Although the CEO is involved to a degree in fund-raising, he or she can count on venture investors to help raise money for the next stage of growth—and hence can concentrate on managing the growth.

Foundations, too, fund only a small percentage of the thousands of needy nonprofit organizations because there is only a limited amount of funding dollars. However, the common practice for foundations is to parcel out those limited dollars to a much higher number of recipients than a venture business would. The result is that a foundation grant covers only a small proportion of a nonprofit's costs. One foundation officer we spoke with put it this way: "We undercapitalize virtually everything we do." Even when a number of grants are combined, most nonprofit organizations are still starved for general operating support. Nonprofit executives, therefore, are forced to spend a large part of their time raising money year after year; some report spending more than half of their time on fund-raising. Under the circumstances, it is not surprising that many nonprofits are not managed well or that good managers may not be attracted to or willing to stay in nonprofit organizations.

LENGTH OF THE RELATIONSHIP

Venture capitalists usually are engaged with a start-up for five to seven years, and some relationships last even longer. That longevity gives them the time to become intimate with the start-up's organizational needs and to find ways to fill them.

Foundations' grant-making time horizons are much shorter and leave little time for nonprofits to develop products, processes, or marketing plans to exploit a new idea. Of the more than 35,000 grants made in 1995 in the five states with the highest number of foundations, only 5.2% were for more than one year. On average, the multi-year grants were only 2.5 years in length. Many foundations simply state that they will not fund any program for more than two or three years. Most of them believe that to offer support for a longer period would make the recipients overly dependent and that nonprofits should become self-sustaining in that time. That line of reasoning has led to foundations' time horizons being out of sync with those of their grantees, which are trying to build organizations that can sustain programs.

THE EXIT

Venture capitalists invest with the understanding that, ultimately, they will sell their stake to a takeout investor. The sale of the venture capitalist's stake effectively ends the formal relationship; it also provides the start-up with an infusion of capital to continue its growth. And, of course, there can be no sale unless the start-up seems to have a strong organization and a viable future.

The nonprofit world has no such mechanism for passing the baton. Few national foundations want to be takeouts for their peers; because of their devotion to innovation, most want to be in on the ground floor. In some instances, foundations are able to structure a series of milestones to govern the release of installments over the life of a large grant. The nonprofit has to demonstrate a new level of performance—operating in a certain number of sites, for example, or serving a certain number of people. But there is often no logical process for one foundation to step back and the next one to step in.

In other instances, foundations will challenge nonprofit organizations to demonstrate that they can sustain a program after a grant terminates. But unlike businesses, nonprofits cannot expect to have investment bankers and their clients waiting to step in with another infusion of capital. Thus when the grant runs out, nonprofit organizations are left to mount a time-consuming search for funds to cover ongoing operation and expansion of programs.

The Next Step: Venture Capital Ideas at Work

Comparing venture capitalists and foundations can be a useful starting point for a reassessment of foundation practices. Such an assessment may yield a new set of practices that foundations can use to build stronger nonprofits. We would like to suggest preliminary queries for foundations and nonprofits to ponder.

QUESTIONS FOR FOUNDATIONS

Foundations can begin the self-assessment by answering the following questions.

Will our grants give nonprofits the organizational support necessary to achieve program goals? If foundations and nonprofits agree in advance on organizational requirements in addition to desired program results, the grant has a much greater chance of having a sustained impact. Hopes for sweeping social change will need to be converted into a series of clear interim results that the grantee and the funder can work toward together.

The GE Fund's College Bound initiative provides a good example. The GE Fund established a clear goal for its education improvement program: to double the number of college-bound students at selected public schools in towns with General Electric Company facilities. It indicated that it would be willing to support local schools over the long term—up to five years in one case—if the schools met certain milestones along the way. As long as the principal is leading the school in new efforts and there are signs of improvement, the GE Fund will stay with the school. GE employees are closely involved in mentoring of students and thus add additional value to the grant. Although the work takes longer and involves more foundation effort, the results have been gratifying, with one school boosting the percentage of college-bound students from 25% to 75%.

What internal capacity do we need to build organizational strength at the nonprofit? Foundation managers and boards will need to reassess their own capacity for a hands-on, organization-centered approach. Many will need additional staff with more experience in organization building to ensure that intelligent bets are made and sound strategies are developed. Foundations can consider recruiting officers with varied backgrounds—in business, institution building, and consulting. The Robin Hood Foundation, for example, has included former management consultants on its staff to help make grants and to deliver management assistance.

In addition to developing in-house managerial expertise, foundations also can give their program officers the authority and the time to respond to the organizational needs of nonprofits. Currently, program officers' workloads are driven by preparation for the next meeting of the board of directors; as a result, program officers have less time to respond to nonprofits. If program officers get more latitude, a closer and more productive bond can be forged between granter and grantee.

Is our grant portfolio too heavy on program innovation at the expense of organization building? According to the *Foundation Grants Index,* general support grants, which can be used for organization building, represented only about 15% of total grants in 1993— down from nearly 25% in 1980. Program grants, meanwhile, grew from just over 30% of all grants made in 1980 to 45% in 1993. Foundations need to determine whether they are invested too heavily in program support to the detriment of organizational capacity.

A group of Philadelphia-based consultants to nonprofits, the Conservation Company, has recommended that funders begin making a new kind of grant—an *organization grant.* The grants would be something between totally unrestricted general support and highly targeted program funds. They could, for example, specify organizational growth targets, as venture capitalists do with private sector start-ups.

In Boston, several foundations have joined with the United Way of Massachusetts Bay and the Massachusetts Department of Public Health to try a new approach to organization building. They have funded the Common Ground project—an intensive three-year program for 17 multiservice, community-based organizations. The funders consider these organizations essential to improving the prospects of several distressed neighborhoods and have therefore moved beyond the traditional quick fix of an organizational assessment and short consultation. Instead, Common Ground will offer the funded organizations ongoing training and professional development plus longer-term consulting resources to help them implement and sustain new approaches. The funders recognize that it is organizational strength that will ultimately determine how successful the programs are.

Foundations might also consider whether they are too wedded to early-stage funding of programs. Many could give support at later stages, when a program or organization is at a critical juncture and other foundations have already invested and left. Later-stage funding, combined with a focus on building organizational capacity, could help nonprofits sharpen their impact.

Are we close enough to nonprofits to help them build organizational strength? Just as foundations' program officers are working more closely with nonprof-

its on program design, so they should be getting closer
to nonprofits on organizational issues. The more that
funders understand the organizational complexity of
nonprofits' work—and shoulder some of the burden and
risk—the better positioned they will be to enhance program impact. Hiring a third-party consultant is a step in
the right direction but does not enable foundations to
understand and fund the appropriate organizational
enhancements.

One promising approach is for foundations to create a separate intermediary organization dedicated to
specialized, long-term work with grantees. A good
example is the New American Schools, based in
Arlington, Virginia. NAS, which is funded with grants
from corporations, foundations, and philanthropists,
was established to give young school-reform programs
what most foundations cannot: large grants over a
long period in conjunction with formal and informal
assistance to expand. Led by a former IBM executive
and a board of corporate CEOs and leading educators, NAS staff members are close enough to their
grantees to offer effective consulting support—such
as developing a quality assurance program—and to
define clear goals for which the grantees can be held
accountable. The capacity building is explicitly understood as a powerful way to deliver and expand programs. The depth of the relationship (NAS works
with only seven programs) enables NAS to act more
like a venture capitalist than like a foundation.

**Are there ways for us to experiment with some
new types of grants?** Foundations can consider experimenting with alternative approaches to grant making

by earmarking a share of their annual outlays for new approaches. For example, foundations could make an unusually long-term grant and see if it results in organizational enhancements and improved programs. Another approach would be to give a few program officers a radically lower caseload to see what they can accomplish with grantees who are eager for a real partnership. Third, foundations might consider partnering with third-party consultants, bringing their capability in-house, and delivering their services along with the grant money.

QUESTIONS FOR NONPROFIT ORGANIZATIONS

Like the foundations that support them, nonprofit organizations need to reconsider their approach to building capacity. Many have been conditioned by the existing grant-seeking process to camouflage their organizational expenses and needs. Nonprofits need to begin articulating compelling organizational strategies and asking foundations to invest in those strategies. Like the foundations, they need to ask themselves a few key questions.

Are we defining our organizational needs for funders? To get more support for organizational needs, a nonprofit will have to articulate a disciplined plan for using the nonprogram money and show how that money will enhance the impact of programs. Instead of worrying about exposing their organizational weaknesses, nonprofits will have to "sell" those weaknesses by explaining that they know where to strengthen their organizations and how to deploy resources efficiently and strategically to get the job done.

When Family Service America, a Milwaukee-based nonprofit, mounted a fund-raising campaign to help the 250 nonprofits in its membership adopt new community-centered approaches, it didn't pitch a new model program. Instead, it laid out an analysis of the members' organizational needs—from training and change management to staff recruiting and benchmarking—and got foundations to invest in organization-strengthening programs as a way of driving program outcomes.

Are we selective about which foundations we want as partners? Although the tendency in fund-raising is to go after any possible grant, getting into an intensive partnership with the wrong venture-type funder is likely to mean wasted effort and considerable angst. Even cash-starved business start-ups are selective about whose venture capital they seek. Nonprofits looking for value-added funding need to communicate clearly where they are trying to take the organization, establish expectations that the funder will share risk and burdens, and create a plan that demands value-added support from a funder. Nonprofits should be wary of foundations that have repositioned themselves under a venture capital banner but lack the capacity, willingness, and patience to do the gritty work.

The venture capital model can show foundations how to help nonprofits build strong organizations.

Are we showing foundations a clear plan that justifies longer-term support? In order to sustain organizational growth, nonprofits need to look beyond the current round of funding. They should propose that early funders stay with them until they are ready for the next stage of funding. One organization that used that approach is Cooperative Home Care Associates (CHCA), a worker-owned cooperative in the New York City borough of the Bronx that provides health care to the elderly in their homes. The cooperative has proved quite successful: it offers home health aides attractive pay, working hours, and benefits, and it offers the community high-quality services. Because of its success, CHCA wanted to expand its operations and launch a training institute to create new cooperatives. When it approached a previous funder—the Charles Stewart Mott Foundation in Flint, Michigan—CHCA presented a long-term plan for building self-sustaining cooperatives. The Mott Foundation subsequently made a series of renewable grants over a seven year period. Programs such as CHCA's provide a clear incentive for funders to move away from traditional terms of one or two years toward the longer-term grants that can have sustained impact.

THE VENTURE CAPITAL MODEL emerged from years of practice and competition. It is now a comprehensive investment approach that sets clear performance objectives, manages risk through close monitoring and frequent assistance, and plans the next stage of funding well in advance. Foundations, although they excel in supporting R&D, have yet to find ways to support their grantees in longer-term, sustainable ways. Because organizational underpinnings were not in place, many innovative programs have not lived up to their initial promise. The venture capital model can act as a starting point for foundations that want to help non-profits develop the organizational capacity to sustain and expand successful programs.

Originally published in March–April 1997
Reprint 97207

Profits for Nonprofits

Find a Corporate Partner

ALAN R. ANDREASEN

Executive Summary

HERE'S A FAMILIAR STORY: A nonprofit organization joins forces with a corporation in a cause-related marketing campaign. It seems like a win-win deal, but the nonprofit—and the media—find out several weeks into the campaign that the corporation's business practices are antithetical to the nonprofit's mission. The nonprofit's credibility is severely damaged.

Is the moral of the story that nonprofits should steer clear of alliances with for-profit organizations? Not at all, Alan Andreasen says. Nonprofit managers can help their organizations avoid many of the risks and reap the rewards of cause-related marketing alliances by thinking of themselves not as charities but as partners in the marketing effort.

More than ever, nonprofits need what many companies can offer: crucial new sources of revenue. But non-

111

profits offer corporate partners a great deal in return: the opportunity to enhance their image—and increase the bottom line—by supporting a worthy cause. Consider the fruitful partnership between American Express and Share Our Strength, a hunger-relief organization. Through the Charge Against Hunger program, now in its fourth year, American Express has helped contribute more than $16 million to SOS. In return, American Express has seen an increase in transactions with the card and in the number of merchants carrying the card.

How can nonprofit managers build a successful partnership? They can assess their organization to see how it can add value to a corporate partner. They can identify those companies that stand to gain the most from a cause-related marketing alliance. And they can take an active role in shaping the partnership and monitoring its progress.

Consider this scenario. At a political fundraiser, the director of a national child-welfare foundation meets the executive vice president of a women's clothing manufacturer. The two start talking about their work. The director describes her organization's efforts to increase the public's awareness of the need for early detection of and intervention in child abuse cases. She tells of her never-ending search for funding and the foundation's inability to reach all the people who need to hear its message. The manufacturing vice president explains that he has been looking for new ways to portray the company as one that is attuned to the needs and concerns of women. Clearly, the two realize, each organization has something very valuable to offer the other.

During the next few months, the foundation and the manufacturing company come up with a plan for a joint campaign against child abuse. The two parties sign a contract stating that the company will underwrite the production of three TV spots, which will run during a six-month period. Both organizations will be identified as sponsors. More than 20 million women are expected to see the spots; half of those women will see them more than once. The foundation's director and the company's CEO are elated. Announcements of the partnership are sent to local affiliates of the foundation, and the media give the story considerable play. The CEO delivers speeches and holds press conferences to tout the company's new strategy and laud its new partner. The foundation's director does the same.

Six weeks into the campaign, the directors of human rights organizations in Bangladesh and Sri Lanka hold a press conference in which they charge the manufacturer with using children in those countries as young as 10 years old to work 12 hours per day making clothes in filthy sweatshops for the equivalent of 20 cents per hour. The directors come to the press conference with videotapes that document the conditions and show the manufacturer's label being sewn into the garments. At the end of the press conference, one of the human rights workers holds up a child-abuse-awareness poster put out by the foundation and says, "This company has joined up with a child welfare organization to make everyone believe that it really wants to end child abuse. Don't fall for it."

Needless to say, the campaign falls apart and the foundation's director is devastated. But her motives in exploring this kind of relationship with a corporation were strategically sound. At a time when society is depending more and more on the nonprofit sector to

provide a social safety net, nonprofit organizations
themselves have been facing tough times. Although total
private giving to charitable organizations, including corporate giving, rose in 1995,
To a corporation, cause- the long-term trend has not
related marketing is not been encouraging. Total pri-
philanthropy. vate giving in constant dollars grew at a snail's pace
from 1990 to 1994. Corporate giving in constant dollars
fell dramatically over the same period. And planned welfare reform will reduce government spending for social
services. In this uncertain environment, nonprofits must
seek new sources of revenue.

The for-profit world is the most obvious and most
promising place to look. In fact, I believe that in order to
survive, nonprofit organizations must develop explicit
ties with for-profit corporations. Instead of hoping to
become the lucky beneficiaries of a company's independent cause-related marketing campaign, such as Benet-
ton's ads promoting AIDS awareness or Ticketmaster's
programs to combat violence, nonprofits must enter
into cause-related marketing alliances with corporations. Such partnerships, of course, are not risk free.
Nonprofits that ally with corporations may find themselves in unproductive short-term relationships and may
end up associated with superficial campaigns and over-
priced and inferior products and services. And, as the
story of the child welfare foundation makes clear, a nonprofit may even find itself linked to a company whose
business practices are completely antithetical to the
nonprofit's mission.

The risks, however, should not deter nonprofits from
pursuing cause-related marketing alliances. Many of the
risks can be avoided if nonprofits think of themselves

not as charities but as true partners in the marketing effort. From the corporation's standpoint, cause-related marketing is not philanthropy. In fact, funding for cause-related marketing programs usually comes out of a company's marketing budget, not its corporate giving or community relations budget. Savvy nonprofit managers will approach cause-related marketing alliances with the same bottom-line mentality. They will assess their organizations' strengths and weaknesses and understand exactly how their organizations can add value to for-profit partners. They will investigate many companies and identify those that stand to gain the most from an alliance. And they will take an active role in shaping a partnership and monitoring its progress at every stage.

How Alliances Work

The tremendous potential of affiliations between nonprofit and for-profit organizations was first recognized by American Express in 1982 when Jerry Welsh, then chief executive officer of worldwide marketing, had an idea for a campaign. The company would donate 5 cents to several arts organizations in San Francisco every time someone used an American Express card in the area and $2 every time someone in the area became a member. The campaign was brief but surprisingly successful. In just three months, American Express contributed $108,000 to the arts organizations and saw a considerable increase in transactions with the card. The company also found that its relationships with participating merchants improved and that more local merchants decided to accept the card.

American Express deemed the campaign so successful that the company decided to try a similar program
on a nationwide basis. In 1983, American Express
promised to donate 1 cent for every transaction with the
card anywhere in the United States, and $1 for each new
card issued during the last quarter of the year, to the
foundation overseeing the renovation of Ellis Island and
the Statue of Liberty. That program, too, was a great
success. Use of the card increased 28% compared with
the same period the previous year, and the company was
able to donate $1.7 million to the renovation project.

Since American Express's pioneering ventures, the
number of alliances between nonprofit and for-profit
organizations has skyrocketed. Avon, American Airlines,
Ocean Spray, Polaroid, Ramada International Hotels &
Resorts, Arm & Hammer, Wal-Mart Stores, and many
other corporations have joined forces with national nonprofit institutions, such as the American Red Cross, the
YMCA, the American Heart Association, and the Nature
Conservancy, as well as local agencies tackling problems
in their communities. It is unusual to go into a super-
market, fast-food restaurant, or drugstore without
encountering posters and other promotional materials
for a social program cosponsored by one or more pri-
vate-sector organizations.

When a corporation and a nonprofit organization
enter into a cause-related marketing alliance, the corporation agrees to undertake a series of actions that will
benefit both the nonprofit and the company. The three
principal kinds of alliance are transaction-based promotions, joint issue promotions, and licensing.

Transaction-based promotions are probably the most
common form of cause-related marketing alliance. In
such an alliance, a corporation donates a specific

amount of cash, food, or equipment in direct proportion to sales revenue—often up to some limit—to one or more nonprofits. American Express's Charge Against Hunger is an excellent example of this type of alliance. The program began in 1993, when the company was looking for ways to motivate cardholders to use their American Express cards and merchants to accept the card. Natalia Cherney Roca, senior director of national marketing, recalls that the employees responsible for developing a new marketing program kept coming back to the successful partnership that American Express had formed with the hunger-relief organization Share Our Strength in 1988. At that time, American Express had agreed to sponsor Taste of the Nation, the largest annual food- and wine-tasting event in the United States, the proceeds of which go to SOS. Hunger relief seemed like the perfect cause for American Express to support because a large proportion of the company's credit-card business comes from use of the card in restaurants and hotels.

As a result of the success of Taste of the Nation and the increasing strength of the relationship between American Express and SOS, American Express decided to elevate its hunger-relief efforts with the annual Charge Against Hunger program. Every time someone uses an American Express card between November 1 and December 31, the company donates 3 cents to SOS, up to a total of $5 million per year. American Express's contributions are augmented considerably by other part-ners that have "joined the charge." For example, in 1994, Kmart agreed to donate 10 cents every time an Ameri-can Express card was used in its stores from November 27 through the end of the year, yielding an additional $250,000. Other promotions during the second year of

the program by the Melville Corporation, Madison
Square Garden, Restaurants Unlimited, and the National
Football League raised more money.

The program has been a great success for both partners. Over the past three years, American Express and
other partners have contributed more than $16 million
to SOS. American
Express has found that
as a result of the pro-
gram, transactions with
the card have increased
and more merchants
now accept the card.

*Hand in Hand, a program
to promote breast health,
will position the corporate
sponsors as organizations
that care about women.*

Furthermore, cardholders have expressed strong support
for the Charge Against Hunger and greater satisfaction
with American Express, and thousands of the company's
employees have volunteered their time to fight hunger.

Joint issue promotions are a second form of cause-
related marketing alliance. In such a partnership, a corporation and one or more nonprofits agree to tackle a
social problem through tactics such as distributing
products and promotional materials, and advertising.
Money may or may not pass between the corporation
and the nonprofit.

A dramatic example of a joint issue promotion is
Hand in Hand, an ongoing program to promote breast
health that was launched in 1992 by *Glamour* magazine
and Hanes Hosiery, and is cosponsored by the National
Cancer Institute, the American College of Obstetricians
and Gynecologists, and the American Health Foundation. The program aims to reach women between the
ages of 18 and 39 through articles in *Glamour*, in-store
promotions sponsored by Hanes, and the production of
a wide range of free educational materials in coopera-

tion with the nonprofit partners, including inserts that eventually will appear in 120 million pairs of hosiery. The sponsors hope that their target audience will not only learn about breast health but also urge their mothers, aunts, and grandmothers—women at much greater risk for breast cancer—to have regular breast exams. A study on four college campuses found that the Hand in Hand materials increased the target population's understanding of and attention to breast health. The program will undoubtedly help *Glamour* and Hanes position themselves as organizations closely attuned to the interests of their target audience.

A third kind of cause-related marketing alliance is the licensing of the names and logos of nonprofits to corporations in return for a fee or percentage of revenues. Licensing predates the emergence of cause-related marketing in the 1980s. Colleges and universities, for example, have licensed

For years, universities have licensed their names and logos. Other nonprofits are now adopting the tactic.

their names and logos for years. Other nonprofits are now adopting the tactic. In April 1996, the American Association of Retired Persons announced that it would begin licensing its name to health maintenance organizations across the United States.

Some nonprofit organizations have been criticized for their licensing arrangements. Consider, for example, the Arthritis Foundation, which decided in 1994 to allow McNeil Consumer Products, a division of Johnson & Johnson, to market a line of four pain relievers called Arthritis Foundation Pain Relievers. In return, the foundation would receive a minimum of $1 million per year from McNeil to finance research. Some organizations,

including consumers' groups, have argued that the
arrangement compromises the foundation's ability to
give unbiased advice, a charge similar to that made
recently against the American Cancer Society, which has
a licensing agreement with SmithKline Beecham for its
NicoDerm CQ nicotine patch. Roy Scott, the Arthritis
Foundation's group vice president for public relations,
acknowledges that the arrangement benefits McNeil
Consumer Products, but he says that the pain relievers
also help arthritis sufferers by enabling the foundation
to communicate to people whom the organization might
not otherwise reach.

The benefits for McNeil in the highly competitive
pain-reliever market are not yet clear, but initial results
have shown that many more people are aware of the
Arthritis Foundation as a result of the sale and promotion of the pain relievers.

The Risks to Nonprofits

Even if a cause-related marketing alliance yields only
minimal returns, what is lost? How bad can the risks be?
The answer is that nonprofit organizations may be
putting themselves at great risk when they join forces
with a corporation, even when the alliance is a great success. Managers of nonprofits must be aware of the risks
in order to adopt a strategy for avoiding them.

WASTED RESOURCES

Building a cause-related marketing alliance requires a
lot of time and effort. What if the venture fails? A corporation can chalk it up to the cost of doing business. A
nonprofit organization, however, which probably has a

small staff and limited resources, may find that it has seriously compromised other activities, such as fundraising, educating people about issues, and building alliances with other corporations and nonprofits.

REDUCED DONATIONS

Cause-related ventures can generate new revenues for nonprofits. But does that mean that total revenues will increase? Not if the organization's traditional donors decide to cut back. People who used to give money to a nonprofit may decide not to if they believe that they have given enough by, for instance, using a credit card issued by a company involved in a transaction-based promotion. Individuals and foundations may reduce their donations if they think that the nonprofit doesn't need their help anymore or if they are turned off by the nonprofit's ties to the for-profit world. And corporations that used to support a nonprofit may take their philanthropy elsewhere if they come to believe that the organization and the issue it promotes have been co-opted by the nonprofit's corporate partner.

But this downside is not inevitable. Studies by American Express suggest that cause-related ventures sometimes can raise the public's awareness of a nonprofit and actually lead to increased donations.

LOSS OF ORGANIZATIONAL FLEXIBILITY

A corporation that enters into an alliance with a nonprofit organization may impose restrictions on the nonprofit. If the restrictions help ensure the expected payoff to the corporation and prevent the nonprofit from engaging in actions that could harm the corporation, they make perfect sense. Nonprofits that enter into a partnership with American Express, for instance, presumably cannot strike a deal with Visa. But suppose one of American Express's nonprofit partners wanted Neiman Marcus to donate $10 for every coat sold in February, after the Charge Against Hunger program had ended. What if American Express accepted the arrangement only if the coat were purchased using an American Express card? A responsible corporate partner like American Express is unlikely to make such demands, but if it does, nonprofits must weigh the benefits of the alliance against possible restrictions on their own fundraising abilities.

TAINTED PARTNERS

Many corporations enter into relationships with nonprofits because they want to bask in the glow of their esteemed partners. When Philip Morris spent $60 million in 1991 to sponsor an exhibit for the 200th anniversary of the Bill of Rights put on by a federal agency, the National Archives, the company was obviously trying to fight off its negative image and lay the foundation for its smokers' rights campaign. The motives behind the donation were transparent, and it is unlikely that the National Archives has suffered by joining forces with a corporation whose marketing strategies many people consider evil.

A tainted corporate partner may prevent a nonprofit from fulfilling its mission.

In some cases, however, a partnership with a tainted for-profit corporation may prevent a nonprofit from carrying out its mission. The child welfare organization described at the beginning of this article, which joined forces with a corporation employing child labor, will most likely have great difficulty collecting funds for its programs in the future. The nonprofit probably could have avoided the fiasco by conducting a thorough examination of the clothing manufacturer. But no amount of research enables a nonprofit to foresee every possible disaster.

ANTITHETICAL MARKETING

A corporate marketer may use tactics that conflict with a nonprofit's image and strategy. In 1994, for example, the American Heart Association entered into an alliance with the makers of several products, including Quaker Oat Squares and Healthy Choice pasta sauce, to distribute a brochure explaining the Food and Drug Administration's new food labels. Almost two-thirds of the brochure was devoted to coupons for the sponsoring products, and many saw the venture as a tawdry gimmick.

OVERWHELMING SUCCESS

A failed alliance can certainly damage a nonprofit organization, but even success presents dangers. One is that the nonprofit will have more funds and more requests for the use of those funds than it can handle. That was one of the concerns that American Express had about its relationship with Share Our Strength. The infusion of money from the Charge Against Hunger program more than tripled SOS's budget. Anticipating that SOS might be overwhelmed as it tried to allocate and monitor the new funds, American Express provided a separate endowment and helped SOS build the necessary administrative systems.

STRUCTURAL ATROPHY

Another potential consequence of a successful cause-related marketing alliance is that the nonprofit will come to rely excessively on corporate funding. What happens if the corporation announces that it will spend its marketing budget in a different way next year and has not helped the nonprofit establish a strong base for fund-raising? In many cases, the nonprofit will have devoted most of its energy and resources to supporting the alliance instead of exploring other potential corporate partners and increasing traditional donations. It may have let its marketing muscles atrophy instead of learning how to sustain the marketing program without corporate support. Finally, it may have relied on its partner to manage contacts with other corporate partners and may have difficulty keeping them on board if the primary sponsor decides to step out.

Becoming a Strategist

Some successful cause-related marketing partnerships are the result of chance encounters at social events. And some fruitful partnerships are developed because a corporate executive or board member has a personal interest in a particular problem or organization. Most alliances that are based on serendipity, however, dissolve before too long.

Nonprofit managers who want partners from the for-profit world must go out and find those partners instead of waiting for corporations to find them. They must develop a strategy that is active rather than reactive. They must become as proficient at marketing their organizations as corporations are at marketing their products and services. In effect, they must become effective strategists.

If nonprofit managers have done their homework, they will understand all the ways in which nonprofits add value to corporate partners, they will have assessed their organizations' strengths and weaknesses, they will have scoped out corporations who might be a good fit, and they will be able to demonstrate to a potential corporate "customer" how the relationship will complement the corporation's long-term strategy.

WHAT KINDS OF VALUE CAN A NONPROFIT ADD?

From a corporate marketer's point of view, a nonprofit organization's most valuable asset is its image. Many companies seeking cause-related marketing alliances hope that a nonprofit's image will define, enhance, or even repair their own.

Consider a study carried out in the fall of 1995 by Roper Starch Worldwide for Cone Communications, a marketing and public relations firm in Boston, Massachusetts. According to interviews with 70 executives at companies engaged in cause-related marketing, the companies used the marketing technique primarily to improve their relationships with customers and enhance their reputations. It seems that the corporate marketers were right to believe that consumers respond to the halo effect. In a survey of nearly 2,000 men and women aged 18 and over conducted by Roper Starch for Cone Communications in August 1993, 31% said that when price and quality are equal, a company's business practices influence their purchases. Fifty-four percent said that they would pay a premium for a product that supports a cause they care about, and 71% said that cause-related marketing is a good way to solve social problems. In particular, companies trying to differentiate themselves in highly competitive markets or attempting to launch a new product or service can gain a great deal from allying themselves with social causes.

A nonprofit can offer a corporation more than its image, however. When a corporation allies itself with a nonprofit, the corporation often saves on advertising and promotional costs because the alliance usually brings free publicity and many public-relations opportunities. The corporation also gains access to the nonprofit's clientele, staff, trustees, and donors, all of whom are potential customers. Such access makes nonprofits with large memberships especially attractive to many companies.

In successful cause-related marketing alliances, the partners have complementary goals.

WHAT ARE OUR ORGANIZATION'S STRENGTHS AND WEAKNESSES?

A nonprofit cannot market itself successfully unless it understands exactly what it can and cannot offer a corporate partner. Managers of nonprofit organizations must ask themselves the following questions:

What is our image? A nonprofit organization with a spotless reputation will be a valuable partner for a corporation with credibility problems. Nonprofits that have been touched by scandal or controversy will have a difficult time developing partnerships until they get their own houses in order.

Do we have strong brand recognition? Corporations that want to be recognized more widely by the public will be most interested in forming partnerships with well-known charities like the Salvation Army and the Muscular Dystrophy Association. A nonprofit that is the darling of the media makes an attractive partner. When television reporters flock to the Special Olympics, for instance, many companies would love their CEOs to be present and their logos prominently displayed.

What do the March of Dimes and Kellogg have in common? Folic acid.

Is our cause especially attractive to certain companies and industries? Every local charity can argue that it seeks to make its community a better place to live and work; thus every corporation located there is a potential partner. The best cause-related marketing alliances, however, emerge when partners have complementary goals and interests. For example, the March of Dimes Birth Defects Foundation wanted more pregnant women to be aware of their need for folic acid, a B vitamin that can help prevent birth defects of the spine and brain. Kellogg wanted to increase sales of Product 19, a breakfast cereal rich in folic acid. The March of Dimes agreed to the use of its name on Product 19 packages in association with a message about folic acid. In return, Kellogg donated $100,000 to the March of Dimes.

Is our target audience particularly appealing to some corporations? A company is likely to give serious consideration to a partnership with a nonprofit organization whose target audience represents a large group of potential customers. A nonprofit that focuses on childhood diseases, for instance, will find natural allies in toy companies or manufacturers of children's clothing.

Do we promote a cause that the public considers especially urgent? Urgent causes generally produce higher payoffs for a corporation than causes on the public's back burner. In a recent document on cause-related marketing, advisers to the American Cancer Society urged corporations seeking cause-related marketing partnerships to ask, "How many people are touched by the cause for which the charity stands, and how strongly are they affected by it?" Some "hot" causes, however, are too hot. For example, many major corporations have shied away from AIDS-related promotions—despite the issue's currency—because they fear that customers would be turned off.

Do we have clout with certain groups of people? Some nonprofit organizations can help corporations gain access to people who influence consumers' purchases. Nonprofit organizations devoted to medical issues, for instance, are highly regarded by health professionals. Such organizations are valuable partners for pharmaceutical companies, who depend on health professionals to prescribe their drugs but often have trouble gaining access to those crucial intermediaries.

Are we local, national, or international? It is extremely valuable for the parties in a cause-related marketing alliance to have similar organizational structures and objectives. Large nonprofits that work on many issues both nationally and locally do best by seeking corporations that can simultaneously conduct national campaigns and work at the local level through divisional offices or franchisees. The National Easter Seal Society, for example, has a national headquarters and many independent local affiliates. The organization has built partnerships with companies that have the same national-local characteristic, such as Safeway, Amway, and Century 21 Real Estate, and thus has been able to raise funds nationally and encourage initiatives by local businesses. Easter Seal raised its level of support from corporations from $3 million in 1980 to $13 million in 1989.

Nonprofits without track records may have to settle for short-term alliances.

In contrast, strictly local organizations should probably avoid a corporation whose focus is national or international. A local women's shelter is best paired with a locally owned retailer or service company.

Do we have a charismatic or well-known leader? Such a leader can guarantee instant media coverage of the alliance and its programs. He or she can also inspire the corporation's employees to participate in the venture. A major asset that Share Our Strength brings to its partnership with American Express is its charismatic leader, Bill Shore, who appears in Charge Against Hunger ads and at events designed to increase support for the program among American Express's employees.

Is our organization experienced and stable? Corporations seeking long-term alliances will look for a nonprofit that has a long track record, sound finances, a sizable staff, and, preferably, experience as a marketing partner. Nonprofits without those credentials may have to settle for short-term alliances.

WHO ARE OUR POTENTIAL PARTNERS?

Once a nonprofit has assessed its strengths and weaknesses and has determined what it can bring to a cause-related marketing alliance, it should assemble an array of potential partners and begin a systematic investigation of each one. No stone should be left unturned. In addition to reviewing annual reports and speeches by corporate leaders, nonprofit managers must talk to as many people as they can. Board members and community leaders often can recommend possible cause-related marketing partners and provide information about them. Those people might even know a company's CEO and other senior executives and thus may have insight into a potentially unfriendly corporate culture or a company's plans to downsize or decrease its support for social programs.

Of course, the most important characteristic to look for in a partner is the extent to which a cause-related marketing program would complement the corporation's goals and eventually increase its bottom line. Other features to look for include the following:

- The corporation clearly recognizes the potential value of a cause-related marketing campaign, which makes marketing the idea of the partnership to the corporation relatively easy.

- The promotion will be a logical—even essential— component of the company's long-term marketing strategy. Partnerships that do not fit a company's strategy and are peripheral to its core interests will ultimately seem superficial to both parties—and perhaps to the public.

- The company does not engage in any business practices that are antithetical to the nonprofit's mission. Think again of the child welfare foundation that unwittingly associated itself with a company that did not support the welfare of children. Nonprofits must learn as much as they can about a potential partner's ethical standards, how strictly the company adheres to those standards, and whether the company extends its ethics to suppliers and to business partners.

- The company's senior executives are enthusiastic about the partnership and will champion it. If the CEO and other senior managers don't think that the program fits the company's strategy, the alliance is unlikely to last.

- The company will devote enough funds and people to the alliance.

- The corporation indicates that it is willing to stick with the initial cause-related marketing campaign for a considerable period.

- The corporation indicates a willingness to continue the partnership beyond the initial campaign.

- The corporation appears eager to involve its employees as well as its suppliers, dealers, and franchisees in the cause-related marketing program. The more ways in which the corporation is connected to the program, the more likely the corporation is to benefit from the partnership and want to continue it.

- The corporation appears unlikely to place undue restrictions on the nonprofit's activities or otherwise interfere with its operations.

Making the Partnership Work

No matter how thoroughly a nonprofit researches potential corporate partners, and no matter how well it markets itself, a cause-related marketing alliance can fail unless both parties start by communicating clearly. In order to negotiate a mutu-
Partners in a ally beneficial alliance, they
marketing alliance must must be explicit about
communicate their goals and expecta-
openly with each other tions. They should spell
and with the public. out—preferably in a con-
tract—the objectives of the project and how they will be measured; whether the corporation will be the nonprofit's only partner or the only partner from a particular industry; and the resources that each party will commit and the areas for which each will be responsible.

As the project gets under way—perhaps on a test basis in one community or in a one-month trial—the partners should meet routinely to track its progress, and they should look at the program's results as honestly as possible. Most of the executives interviewed by Roper Starch for Cone Communications in 1995 said that their companies did not measure cause-related programs primarily in terms of direct sales. Instead, the companies tracked improvements in their image and increases in customer loyalty and in the satisfaction of employees and customers. Some effects of cause-related marketing programs, such as the long-term consequences for a company's image, are difficult to measure. And there is always the danger that either party will want to put a positive spin on soft data. A partnership will have the best chance of enduring if both sides are candid about their measures. Candor builds trust and increases the likelihood that midcourse corrections will be made in a flagging venture.

Both partners must also communicate openly and honestly with the public. Many good programs can be sabotaged if the public believes that a company is using a nonprofit's positive image to disguise an inferior product, that the nonprofit is being manipulated by the corporation, or that the nonprofit will not actually receive funds from the program. For example, if there is a cap on corporate contributions in a transaction-based promotion, that should be clear from the start. If corporate contributions are unrelated to consumers' actions, the public must be told.

Nonprofit alliances can be difficult to manage. But when they work, they can have great payoffs for both partners—as well as for the public. While a corporation is boosting its image and a nonprofit is securing crucial funds, both parties are also focusing attention on social problems that might otherwise be neglected. Cause-related marketing is about marketing, but it is also about finding new ways to improve people's lives.

Originally published in November–December 1996
Reprint 96601

Enterprising Nonprofits

J. GREGORY DEES

Executive Summary

FACED WITH RISING COSTS, more competition for fewer donations and grants, and increased rivalry from for-profit companies entering the social sector, nonprofits are turning to the commercial arena to leverage or replace their traditional sources of funding. The drive to become more businesslike, however, holds many dangers for nonprofits. In the best of circumstances, nonprofits face operational and cultural challenges in the pursuit of commercial funding. In the worst, commercial operations can undercut an organization's social mission. To explore the new possibilities of commercialization and to avoid its perils, nonprofit leaders need to craft their strategies carefully. A framework—what the author calls the *social enterprise spectrum*—can help such leaders understand and assess their options.

Nonprofits first must identify potential sources of earned income; then they should set clear and realistic financial objectives. Commercial programs don't need to be profitable to be worthwhile. They can instead improve the efficiency and the effectiveness of organizations by reducing the need for donated funds; by providing a more reliable, diversified funding base; and by enhancing the quality of programs by instilling market discipline. In the end, commercial operations will not—and should not—drive out philanthropic initiatives. But thoughtful innovation in the social sector is essential if organizations are to leverage limited philanthropic resources.

Last august, the American Medical Association backed out of an exclusive deal with Sunbeam Corporation, a manufacturer of such health-related products as thermometers and blood pressure monitors. The deal would have allowed Sunbeam to display an AMA seal of approval on some of its products—products that would then be packaged with AMA-sponsored health information. In return, Sunbeam would pay a royalty to the AMA on sales of the endorsed products.

The agreement sparked an outcry from the AMA's members and other observers who feared that it would compromise the integrity of the 150-year-old association. The reaction was so strong that the AMA's board of trustees was forced to rescind key terms of the deal just one week after announcing it. The revised policy specified that the association would not endorse products, accept royalties, or enter into exclusive arrangements with corporate partners. Sunbeam would be asked only to distribute the AMA's health information with its products and would pay the association only enough to cover the costs of producing the inserts. The AMA would not profit from the corporate use of its name.

The AMA's experience highlights how turbulent the new tide of commercialization in the nonprofit world can be. Faced with rising costs, more competition for fewer donations and grants, and increased rivalry from for-profit companies entering the social sector, nonprofits are turning to the for-profit world to leverage or replace their traditional sources of funding. In addition, leaders of nonprofits look to commercial funding in the belief that market-based revenues can be easier to grow and more resilient than philanthropic funding.

The drive to become more businesslike, however, holds many dangers for nonprofits. In the best of circumstances, nonprofits face operational and cultural challenges in the pursuit of commercial funding. In the worst, commercial operations can undercut an organization's social mission. To explore the new possibilities of commercialization and to avoid its perils, nonprofit leaders need to craft their strategies carefully. A framework—what I call the *social enterprise spectrum*—can help them understand and assess the options they face.

The Rising Tide of Commercialization

Nonprofit organizations have traditionally operated in the so-called social sector to solve or ameliorate such problems as hunger, homelessness, environmental pollution, drug abuse, and domestic violence. They have also provided certain basic social goods—such as education, the arts, and health care—that society believes the marketplace by itself will not adequately supply. Nonprofits have supplemented government activities, contributed ideas for new programs and other innovations, and functioned as vehicles for private citizens to pursue their own visions of the good society independent of government policy. Although some nonprofits have relied heavily on fees—especially those in the fields of health care and education—government grants and private donations have also accounted for a considerable portion of the funding that many nonprofits receive.

An increasing number of nonprofits are seeking additional revenues by behaving more like for-profit organizations.

Recently, however, an increasing number of nonprofits have been seeking additional revenues by behaving more like for-profit organizations. Some are raising funds through auxiliary commercial enterprises. For example, Save the Children, an international development agency, sells a line of men's neckwear. Such ventures are for the most part bold, creative extensions of the old-fashioned bake sale or car wash: they get the word out about a nonprofit organization and its cause and, if successful, generate cash.

A new pro-business zeitgeist has made for-profit initiatives more acceptable in the nonprofit world.

More dramatically, a number of nonprofits are beginning to commercialize the core programs through which they accomplish their missions; that is, they are looking for ways to make these programs rely less on donations and grants and more on fees and contracts. Some are accepting contracts from government agencies, for instance, to run social service programs, schools, and job-training programs for welfare recipients. Others are performing fee-based work for corporations or are charging beneficiaries directly for services that used to be free. For example, universities are engaging in contract research and are forming commercial partnerships to capitalize on the results of their noncontract research. Better Business Bureaus have explored charging a fee for reports on companies. Some nonprofits are even launching business enterprises to serve the objectives of their missions. For instance, San Francisco's Delancy Street Restaurant, run by the Delancy Street Foundation, is staffed by ex-convicts and former substance abusers who participate in Delancy's intensive self-help program and work in the restaurant as part of their rehabilitation. Finally, a few nonprofits, most notably hospitals and health maintenance organizations, are converting to for-profit status or are being acquired by for-profit companies.

Nonprofit leaders are scrambling to find commercial opportunities for a number of reasons. First, a new pro-business zeitgeist has made for-profit initiatives more acceptable. With the apparent triumph of capitalism worldwide, market forces are being widely celebrated. And with growing confidence in the power of competition and the profit motive to promote efficiency and innovation, many observers are suggesting that market discipline should exert more influence in the social sector—especially when those observers have fundamental doubts about the performance of social enterprises.

Second, many nonprofit leaders are looking to deliver social goods and services in ways that do not create dependency in their constituencies. Even many advocates for the poor or disadvantaged believe that institutional charity can undermine beneficiaries' self-esteem and create a sense of helplessness. As a result, some organizations are charging beneficiaries for at least a portion of the cost of services. Others seek to use business as a tool for helping people develop self-reliance and build marketable capabilities. One important study of nonprofit businesses that help the homeless and other disadvantaged groups become self-sufficient was recently published by Jed Emerson of the Roberts Foundation (now called the Roberts Enterprise Development Fund and originally created by George Roberts of the LBO firm, Kholberg, Kravis, and Roberts). The study documents a host of job-creating nonprofit businesses—such as bakeries, ice cream shops, and greeting-card and silk-screened T-shirt stores—all in the San Francisco Bay Area.

Third, nonprofit leaders are searching for the holy grail of financial sustainability. They view earned-income-generating activities as more reliable funding sources than donations and grants. Many of them now consider extensive dependency on donors as a sign of weakness and vulnerability. Self-funding is the new mantra. At a minimum, organizations seek a diversity of funding sources to provide a cushion in case one source declines or disappears. Commercial funding is particularly attractive because it is potentially unrestricted: owners of a commercial enterprise can use excess revenues for whatever purposes they like, whereas the use of grants and donations to nonprofits is often restricted to particular projects and purposes. Furthermore, commercial markets are potentially huge.

Fourth, the sources of funds available to nonprofits are shifting to favor more commercial approaches. Competition for philanthropic dollars is intense, but money is becoming available for operating on a more commercial basis. Consider the following changes: Today few foundations want to provide ongoing funding—even to highly successful projects. Most choose to limit their funding to short periods in an effort to press grantees to become increasingly self-sufficient. At the same time, government agencies are shifting from providing services themselves to contracting with

Like the proverbial tail wagging the dog, commercial funding can pull a nonprofit away from its social mission.

independent nonprofit and for-profit organizations. Such contracting creates opportunities, but government grant programs are being cut or threatened. Finally, corporations are thinking more strategically about philanthropy. They are no longer deciding where their grant dollars will go solely on the merits of the programs they will fund but on the value they will derive from the relationship with a particular nonprofit. Some corporations are exploring the benefits of direct business relationships with nonprofits, and others have started paying for social services as an employee benefit—again creating new commercial opportunities in the social sector.

Fifth, competitive forces are leading nonprofit managers to consider commercial alternatives to traditional sources of funding. New for-profit companies have made considerable headway in health care and are beginning to enter other social services—such as running orphanages, managing charter schools, and providing welfare-to-work programs. As for-profit companies enter an industry and some nonprofits start experimenting with commercial operations, other nonprofits feel pressured to follow the lead of their competitors that are turning to commercial sources of revenue. For instance, many nonprofit hospitals mimic the management styles and methods of their for-profit counterparts. Similarly, if some major universities subsidize their operations by commercializing research, others will do the same—if only to maintain a competitive cost structure. Once commercialization in a social-sector industry begins, many nonprofits jump on the bandwagon—even if questions remain about how successful those operations ultimately will be.

Navigating Dangerous Currents

Market-based funding approaches do have an important role to play in the social sector. If those social programs that are able to generate their own income in fact do so, philanthropic dollars can be allocated to activities that truly need to be subsidized. But embracing commercial opportunities can be risky. The often perilous currents of commercialization in the social sector must be navigated with care. There are a number of dangers that nonprofit leaders should be aware of.

Like the proverbial tail wagging the dog, new sources of revenue can pull an organization away from its original social mission. Consider the YMCA. The association today generates substantial revenues by operating health-and-fitness facilities for middle-class families, but critics charge that the YMCA has lost sight of its mission to promote the "spiritual, mental, and social condition of young men." Similarly, a former board member of a major dance company resigned because he felt the company had neglected its artistic mission and had become too commercial by performing popular pieces to generate revenue. Of course, changing a mission in order to ensure the survival of a worthwhile organization may be justifiable. But nonprofits should be aware that by seizing market opportunities, they may be drawn incrementally and unintentionally into new arenas far from their original focus.

Nonprofit leaders should also recognize that creating a sustainable and profitable business is not easy. Market discipline can be harsh. Some studies indicate that more than 70% of new businesses fail within eight years of their inception. Substantial profits, although not impossible to achieve, are hard to come by. In perfectly competitive markets, companies make only enough to cover costs and to compensate capital providers adequately. Running a profitable business requires skill, luck, and flexibility. Nonprofits may have some advantages when competing in commercial markets. Those advantages include their tax status and their ability to capitalize on volunteer labor, to attract in-kind donations and supplier discounts, and to use philanthropic money to help cover start-up costs and capital investments. But those advantages alone will not ensure profitability.

Many nonprofits simply do not have the business-specific organizational skills, managerial capacity, and credibility to succeed in commercial markets. And building new organizational capabilities can be costly and difficult. Hiring people with business skills and market focus is not enough. An organization must be receptive to and supportive of new activities; it also must be able to integrate the skills and values of the new staff. Many MBAs who go to work in nonprofit organizations find themselves ostracized by their colleagues. One business school graduate and former brand manager at a major corporation, who now heads a division of a nonprofit devoted to environmental protection, spent several years overcoming the skepticism of core staff members. In that organization, scientific credentials and a demonstrated commitment to the environment were signs of prestige; business skills were suspect. The division head's staff feared that he would focus on the bottom line to the exclusion of the mission.

Indeed, the culture of commerce can conflict with that of the social sector in several ways. Many who work in nonprofits are uncomfortable with the style of operations common to for-profit organizations. Consider the conflicts that occurred at a major nongovernmental organization operating in a developing country. On one side were the social workers who were committed to helping their poverty-stricken clientele. On the other side were the loan officers in the newly formed, self-sustaining microloan operation, which helps some of the same clients start small businesses. When the loan officers had to demand payments from a client, the social workers objected. They found this kind of businesslike behavior offensive; it ran counter to their sense of compassion. Although nonprofits have become more accepting of business in general, some nonprofit managers still bristle at the use of business language. Even the word *customer* can put people off. The leader of one community-based arts organization, uncomfortable with the idea of being customer driven, contends that her mission is to provide a forum for avant-garde African-American playwrights, not to cater to the tastes of a local audience. And she is far from unique. Social workers, curators, educators, doctors, nurses, artists, scientists, and other professionals who staff nonprofits may balk when they are expected to adapt more to businesslike methods of operation.

Commercialization can also undermine the role a nonprofit organization plays in its community. Community-based nonprofits often serve as outlets for citizens to act on their philanthropic impulses—to join voluntarily in efforts to improve the conditions of their community. The executive director of a major food bank believes that the mission of his organization is not only to supply food for the needy but also to provide opportunities for people from all walks of life to volunteer, to serve the poor, and to interact with one another. Volunteers may not be so ready to contribute their time to for-profit programs. Although commercialization need not drive out philanthropic activities, the two impulses can be difficult to balance.

When nonprofits become more businesslike, they may run afoul of public values and meet with political resistance. For instance, the Red Cross blood-bank system has come under attack recently for its attempt to create a national system of distribution, its allegedly aggressive pursuit of donors, and its alleged failure to serve hospitals that favor other blood providers. Of course, the Red Cross has defended itself against those charges, but the point is that nonprofits are not expected to behave like businesses. When they do, critics are ready to pounce.

Nonprofits that undertake commercial initiatives also face resistance from for-profit competitors. Nonprofits are perceived to have the unfair advantages of tax breaks and lower costs for labor, capital, and supplies. Cross-sector competition exists in industries from day care to publishing to gift catalogs. For-profit providers of adult education services complain about nonprofit rivals. Local retailers don't like competing with university-owned stores that sell not only textbooks but also clothing, computers, records—items that have little to do with a school's educational mission. If the competition continues to heat up, for-profit rivals will step up the pressure for a reconsideration of the tax exemptions offered to nonprofits.

Charting a Favorable Course

Despite the risks of commercialization, nonprofit leaders can chart a favorable course through commercial waters in their search for ways both to reduce their organizations' dependence on grants and to enhance their mission-related performance. The challenge is to find a financial structure that reinforces the organization's mission, uses scarce resources efficiently, is responsive to changes, and is practically achievable.

To begin, nonprofit leaders must understand the full range of available options. A social enterprise is commercial to the extent that it operates like a business in how it acquires its resources and distributes its goods and services. The more commercial an organization, the less it relies on philanthropy. Few social enterprises can or should be purely philanthropic or purely commercial; most should combine commercial and philanthropic elements in a productive balance. Many already do. (See the exhibit "The Social Enterprise Spectrum," which shows the range of commercialization in terms of a nonprofit's relationships with its key stakeholders.)

For instance, colleges and universities charge a tuition that does not cover operating costs because such institutions can draw on alumni donations, research grants, and income from endowments. Some nonprofits cross-subsidize one program or client group with another. Many day care centers use a sliding fee scale so that wealthier families subsidize poorer ones. Ballet companies often use profits from holiday performances of the *Nutcracker* to support artistically important but unprofitable productions. Still other nonprofits obtain funding from third-party payers, such as governments and corporations. Health care providers commonly receive the bulk of their revenues from public and private insurance plans. Social service providers can contract with state government agencies to provide their services to state residents.

As they evaluate their organizations' potential to operate at the commercial end of the spectrum, nonprofit leaders should begin by identifying all potential

The Social Enterprise Spectrum

		Purely Philanthropic	◄─────►	Purely Commercial
Motives, Methods, and Goals		Appeal to goodwill	Mixed motives	Appeal to self-interest
		Mission driven	Mission and market driven	Market driven
		Social value	Social and economic value	Economic value
Key Stakeholders	Beneficiaries	Pay nothing	Subsidized rates or mix of full payers and those who pay nothing	Market-rate prices
	Capital	Donations and grants	Below-market capital, or mix of donations and market-rate capital	Market-rate capital
	Workforces	Volunteers	Below-market wages, or mix of volunteers and fully paid staff	Market-rate compensation
	Suppliers	Make in-kind donations	Special discounts, or mix of in-kind and full-price donations	Market-rate prices

commercial sources of revenue. Potential paying customers include the organization's intended beneficiaries, third parties with a vested interest in the mission, and others for whom the organization can create value.

EARNED INCOME FROM INTENDED BENEFICIARIES

In an ideal world, social enterprises would receive funding and attract resources only when they produced their intended social impact—such as alleviating poverty in a given area, reducing drug abuse, delivering high-quality education, or conserving natural resources. The best strategy in this ideal world would be to ask the intended beneficiaries to pay full cost for services. After all, the beneficiary would be in a prime position to determine if the value created was sufficiently high to justify the costs of creating it. In the real world, however, this approach works only for nonprofits that are in the business of serving a clearly defined and well-informed consumer who is able to pay. Membership organizations are one example; their beneficiaries, or members, pay for services through membership fees.

Commercialization can often change the character of a nonprofit's relationship with its beneficiaries.

Few nonprofits will be able to reduce their missions to that kind of formula. The intended beneficiaries of a social enterprise are rarely well-informed, viable, or appropriate payers. In some instances, it isn't even clear who the intended beneficiaries are. Who is the intended beneficiary of a project to save the whales from extinc-

tion? The whales? The general public? Future generations? In many social enterprises, the intended beneficiary is unable to pay anything close to the cost of the
services delivered. For instance, if development agencies
such as CARE, Save the Children, and Oxfam—agencies
that serve poor, distressed communities—relied exclusively on fees charged to residents, they would be able to
operate only in relatively wealthy communities.

In other instances, beneficiaries may not be sufficiently knowledgeable to make an informed purchase
decision. Or they may not fully appreciate the value of
the service being offered. For example, abusive spouses
who recognize that they have a problem but underesti-
mate its severity might not realize the benefit of counseling to themselves and to their families until after they
have gone through a program. If full payment were
required, they might not undergo counseling at all.
Because collective goods are often at stake in the work
of nonprofits, society might lose in such an exchange as
well. For example, society benefits from the drop in
crime rates that occurs if addicts are treated in rehabilitation programs; but if addicts were required to pay the
full cost of the program, few would join.

Finally, requiring intended beneficiaries to pay may
be inappropriate, even when it is feasible. Commercialization can often change the character of a nonprofit's
relationship with its beneficiaries. Imagine Amnesty
International charging a fee to the political prisoners
who are released as a result of its activities or the Red
Cross charging disaster victims for relief services. If Big
Brothers and Big Sisters charged children or their families for a mentor's time, wouldn't the child suspect that
the mentor was there simply for the pay, and wouldn't
that suspicion undermine the relationship?

To understand the full range of commercial options, nonprofit leaders should evaluate potential revenues for all beneficiary groups, services, and products. Assumptions about the viability and appropriateness of charging for services also should be explored and questioned. For instance, should a group that serves people with disabilities assume that its constituency could not or should not pay for any of the services it provides? In fact, it can be demeaning to treat people with disabilities as charity cases. Asking for at least some payment can give beneficiaries a sense of responsibility and enhance their commitment to the treatment. In programs requiring the active participation of beneficiaries, pricing serves to screen out those who are not sufficiently serious about the program. If the intended beneficiaries vary in their ability to pay, nonprofit leaders should examine the feasibility and desirability of cross-subsidization and discounted fees. The organization could use sliding fee scales, scholarships, special discounts, and other devices to allow access to people of lesser means. It could also opt for deferred payments along the lines of student loans for higher education. A more radical alternative to deferred payments would be to encourage prepayment or group payment using membership fees or an insurance scheme. Some colleges already offer to guarantee tuition rates many years into the future if parents pay tuition in advance.

EARNED INCOME FROM THIRD-PARTY PAYERS WITH A VESTED INTEREST

Faced with the difficulties of charging intended beneficiaries for services rendered, social enterprises often need to search for next-best solutions. To that end, nonprofits can look to third-party funding sources. The most likely direct payers are government agencies and corporations that have a vested interest in an intended beneficiary group or in the enterprise's mission. The government's role as a source of revenue for certain nonprofit organizations is widely recognized. It has a vested interest in collective goods and in the welfare of the poor. Corporations play a similar role when they subsidize such employee benefits as health care, day care, elder care, family counseling, and alcohol and drug rehabilitation.

Third-party payment can take many forms. The payers can issue vouchers to be used at the discretion of the beneficiary, can reimburse for services chosen by beneficiaries, or can contract directly for service delivery. Contracting itself can range from cost plus to flat rates per capita. In many cases, the beneficiaries share some of the costs through co-payments and deductibles. This approach appealed to the founders of GuateSalud, a health maintenance organization for the rural working poor in Guatemala. After struggling to raise donations for their work, the founders decided to market their health services to the owners of small coffee plantations who employ poor migrant workers during the harvest season. The owners paid a monthly fee for the service, and workers paid token fees for visits to the health facility and for pharmaceuticals. The arrangement was a success: the owners got a healthier workforce, and the workers gained access to medical care and health education that otherwise would not have been available to them.

Nonprofit leaders considering this option need to ask how closely the interests of third-party payers align with the organization's mission. If the interests diverge from

the mission now or in the future, how can the mission
be protected? The challenge nonprofit leaders face, then,
is to find third parties whose interests fit the enterprise's
mission and to maximize that alignment. They need to
conduct a thorough, fact-based assessment to determine
the impact of potential arrangements on the mission.
For instance, if it is important for GuateSalud to
improve the overall health of poor native Guatemalans,
is contracting with the plantation owners, who have
access to many of those workers only during harvest,
enough? The answer to that question depends in large
part on whether a brief health intervention at harvest
time makes a significant difference in health outcomes.
The question also must be weighed in the context of
alternatives: if funding isn't available for a more substantial intervention, such as placing clinics in remote
regions or having health providers travel extensively,
contracting with the owners may be better than
nothing.

As they conduct their assessment, nonprofit leaders
should also consider such practical matters as the costs
of negotiating contracts and managing the ongoing relationship with a third-party payer. In some cases, particularly in the case of government contracting, the nonprofit can incur considerable incremental administrative
costs.

Finally, nonprofit leaders should evaluate how reliable the revenue stream will be over time. It can be risky
for a nonprofit to have just one or a few major payers
because a canceled contract would be a major blow to
the organization. For instance, Leeway, a nursing home
for people with AIDS, depends heavily on Connecticut
Medicaid reimbursements. A change in state policy
could prevent Leeway from fulfilling its mission. A single

funding source may be the best available to an organization such as Leeway, but leaders need to consider the associated risks. Changing funding sources can be quite disruptive and can require a great deal of management time. Yet, some disruptions may be necessary, considering that the alternative—philanthropic fund-raising—is also very time consuming and uncertain.

EARNED INCOME FROM OTHERS

In addition to obtaining direct payments for mission-related services, nonprofits can receive indirect sources of earned income from third parties. One common form of indirect commercial support is advertising. Corporations may pay for the right to promote their products to a nonprofit's target market. For instance, companies that make baby products might sponsor an educational program for mothers of low-birth-weight infants. So-called cause-related marketing, in which a company uses its support of a nonprofit cause in its promotions, is an extension of this idea. In addition, nonprofits can use their name recognition to *co-brand* products, such as pain relievers endorsed by the Arthritis Foundation. Businesses and individuals also can indirectly support social enterprises by purchasing goods and services. Local hotels and hospitals might contract for services from a commercial laundry operated by a homeless shelter to provide job training and income to residents. In such a case, the third parties are paying the shelter not to provide training for homeless people but to provide laundry services; in other words, they are paying the shelter indirectly to serve its primary constituency.

Finding indirect sources of revenue often requires creativity. Nonprofit leaders should ask themselves how their organizations could create value for someone who would pay. Because this source of earned income is the one least directly related to mission performance, it can risk pulling the organization off course by diverting valuable management resources away from activities related to the organization's core mission. As a result, leaders need to be particularly careful to question the appropriateness of this kind of financial relationship. Will the demands of running a competitive commercial laundry create pressure to employ only shelter residents who already have good job skills, those least in need of training? When corporations with vested interests pay for research, will universities shift resources from basic science to more applied areas? Will they become scientific advocates for the interests of their paying clients?

Nonprofits should keep in mind that commercial programs don't need to be profitable to be worthwhile.

Choosing the Right Vessel

Once nonprofits identify potential sources of earned income, they should set clear and realistic financial objectives. Commercial programs don't need to be profitable to be worthwhile. They can improve the efficiency and effectiveness of the organization by reducing the need for donated funds, by providing a more reliable, diversified funding base, or by enhancing the quality of programs by instilling market discipline. Following are the possible financial approaches that a nonprofit might adopt. They move roughly from left to right on the social enterprise spectrum.

FULL PHILANTHROPIC SUPPORT

After reviewing their options, the leaders of a nonprofit might decide that no potential sources of earned income are appealing, given the organization's mission and values. They must then decide on the right mixture of philanthropic sources: cash donations, in-kind donations, and volunteer labor. Very few nonprofits will be staffed solely by volunteers and will acquire all their equipment, facilities, and supplies as in-kind donations. For most organizations, cash donations provide a way to adopt more commercial labor and purchasing practices. For instance, a mentoring program for disadvantaged youth could have a paid staff, volunteer adult mentors, some in-kind donations, and a variety of cash operating expenses, and could rely exclusively on grants and donations to cover all out-of-pocket costs. Many new and small social-service nonprofits operate this way, with negligible or no earned income.

PARTIAL SELF-SUFFICIENCY

Other nonprofits might conclude that the sources of earned income available to them will cover only part of their necessary operating expenses, even when taking into account potential in-kind donations and volunteer labor. They will need cash donations to pay for some out-of-pocket operating expenses, as well as for start-up costs and capital investments. Most institutions of higher education operate this way. Tuition covers only a portion of total costs; donors subsidize the rest. The difficulty such organizations face is determining the right level of subsidy. To determine that level, they must assess not only potential commercial and philanthropic revenues but also competitive dynamics, values, and mission-related objectives.

For example, Berea College in Berea, Kentucky, targets financially needy Appalachian students and charges no tuition. All students work, but the college covers its costs largely through income from a sizable endowment and annual giving. In contrast, Vermont's Bennington College decided from the start that it did not want to be beholden to donors who might interfere with its mission. (Bennington was founded as an experimental college for women and emphasized individualized, nontraditional courses of study.) The college did not run annual fund-raising campaigns and built a negligible endowment. Instead, it charged a high tuition; in fact, its tuition was frequently one of the highest in the nation.

Both schools have long delivered high-quality education. So which model is best? The answer to that question depends both on how well the model serves the institution's mission and on the model's feasibility for sustaining its institution. Bennington's model would not have worked for Berea's mission serving the Appalachian poor. For a time in the 1980s and early 1990s, it did not work very well for Bennington's mission either. High costs and competition for students made the pay-as-you-go model difficult to maintain. The college recently restructured and has launched a capital campaign to build an endowment, but Bennington will not need an endowment as large as Berea's.

CASH FLOW SELF-SUFFICIENCY

Many nonprofit social enterprises want commercial revenues but not market-based costs. They use earned income to cover out-of-pocket operating expenses, but the costs they incur are lower than market rates because of their ready access to philanthropic investment capital (such as grants and below-market program-related investments made by foundations), volunteers (or below-market wages), and in-kind donations (or discounts). Such organizations are technically self-funding and may even generate excess cash to cover the costs of strapped mission-related activities, but they still depend on noncash philanthropic subsidies.

Help the World See (HTWS) and the new permanent eye-care clinics it has established in developing countries illustrate how this model works. When HTWS began, it sent volunteer doctors with donated glasses to developing countries to set up temporary clinics. Then five years ago, the organization embarked on a new strategy. It would establish permanent clinics, offering affordable ongoing eye care, that would operate self-sufficiently on a cash-flow basis. Start-up capital would be donated; in-kind space would be provided by governments or sympathetic nongovernmental organizations; materials to produce glasses would be acquired at a discount from willing suppliers; and staff training would be covered by grants. But the organization would pay the staff and cover out-of-pocket operating expenses by charging a small fee for glasses. The new strategy demanded a trade-off: the stand-alone clinics would not be able to serve—at least not initially—the very poorest residents, who could not afford even the small fee for glasses. (It was hoped that one day the clinics would be able to generate a "profit" to pay for services for the very poor.) But the clinics could still serve many who were not able to find or afford glasses any other way.

OPERATING EXPENSE SELF-SUFFICIENCY

Nonprofits may be able to have earned income cover all operating expenses, even if those expenses are at market rates. They might obtain donations or below-market loans to cover some start-up expenses and capital expenditures, but after that, the operation would stand on its own without relying on additional philanthropy of any kind, including volunteer and in-kind donations. Few social ventures launched by nonprofits can aspire to this degree of independence from philanthropic support when it comes to operations. One example of a non-profit organization that has adopted this model is the Kentucky Highlands Investment Corporation. It began with nearly $15 million in grants from the federal gov-ernment to use as venture capital to stimulate economic development in several distressed counties in southeast-ern Kentucky. Using returns from its investments, the corporation has been able to cover its operating costs for the venture fund and to make new investments—in the process preserving the value of the fund.

Even when operating self-sufficiency is the goal, most new ventures will need some form of cash subsidy dur-ing the start-up period. But nonprofit leaders must decide how long to subsidize the venture. Cutting one's losses in mission-related operations can be difficult: when a new program cannot stand on its own, a non-profit may have to decide whether to continue the pro-gram even though it will need to be subsidized. Shutting down a program may have political costs or an unfortu-nate impact on an organization's mission. For instance, the Bangladesh Rural Advancement Committee (BRAC) created a silk industry from scratch in Bangladesh to employ women and the landless poor. BRAC intended

for all parts of the industry's value chain—from growing
mulberry trees to selling the products made with BRAC
silk—to operate self-sufficiently. But the silk-reeling
plants were very inefficient, in large part because of the
inherently poor quality of the cocoons that were bred
to grow in Bangladesh. To pay its workers a living wage,
BRAC had to accept losses on this stage in the production process. Shutting down the plants would have
crippled the entire silk project, hurting thousands of
workers and strengthening the hand of BRAC's fund-
amentalist political opponents. BRAC intends to work to
make the plants profitable, but it will be difficult to pull
the plug on this operation even if profitability is never
achieved.

FULL-SCALE COMMERCIALIZATION

When an organization is fully commercial, revenue covers all costs at market rates, including the market cost of
capital, without a hint of philanthropic subsidy even for
start-up expenses. The organization repays start-up capital at a market rate of return and is sufficiently profitable to attract new investment capital for expansion.
Few nonprofits can achieve full-scale commercialization.
Because nonprofits cannot accept equity investments
and it is difficult to be financed totally with debt, such
organizations often are structured as, or convert to, for-
profit enterprises.

Nonprofits that are this strongly committed to
commercialization—and to their independence from
philanthropic subsidies—face a challenging balancing
act. On the one hand, they will need to act like businesses by preserving their flexibility and by being
willing to cut losses and search for new sources of

revenue. On the other hand, they will have to do so within the constraints of their mission. Absent a philanthropic cushion and a commitment to philanthropic supporters, nonprofit leaders will need to keep the enterprise's mission in mind when reacting to business pressures.

MIXED ENTERPRISES

Finally, it should be noted that many social enterprises are actually multi-unit operations that run programs with different financial objectives and funding structures. A major museum might have both a profitable catalog business and a highly subsidized research-and-acquisition operation. The Nature Conservancy established a for-profit company, the Eastern Shore Sustainable Development Corporation, in order to generate profits and create jobs while protecting the environment. The conservancy has partnered with for-profit companies such as Georgia Pacific to find profitable ways to conserve natural habitats, and it offers ecological travel programs for a fee to its members. Yet many of its core conservation activities still rely heavily on donations. (See the insert "Related Readings" on page 165.)

Other multi-unit social enterprises are for-profit organizations with nonprofit affiliates. Shorebank Corporation, for instance, is a development bank with a social mission. It has commercial-banking and real estate operations, as well as an affiliate nonprofit community-development corporation that is dependent on grants. The corporation as a whole has benefited from obtaining program-related capital investments at below-market rates from foundations but otherwise has very commercial methods of operation.

The Skills Needed to Sail Commercial Waters

If nonprofits are to explore commercial options, it is essential both that they build business capabilities and that they manage organizational culture. Management skills are important for all nonprofit organizations, but commercialization calls for expertise, knowledge, and attitudes more commonly found in the business world. Nonprofit managers need to become trained in business methods if they are to explore commercial options effectively. One way to gain such training is to reach out for help. Nonprofit managers can begin in their own backyards by finding more effective ways to draw on board members with relevant business experience. The resulting exchange will be a learning experience for both parties. Business board members are often an underutilized source of management expertise, and they need coaching and coaxing to adapt their business frameworks to the context of a social enterprise. They must understand the risks of becoming too businesslike and of moving too quickly. Nonprofit leaders also can reach out for pro bono consulting from volunteer businesspeople or from business school students. And nonprofits exploring commercialization can form alliances with for-profit companies to provide complementary skills and training in business methods.

Without internal staff expertise, however, the advice of board members, consultants, and partners may not be worth much. The organization needs staff that can understand and implement the new agenda. Organizations can hire employees with business skills, but they will need to address the cultural conflicts and compensation problems that could arise. The new hires must be supported fully, and care must be taken to allow them to build credibility within the core culture. Nonprofit leaders should anticipate cultural conflict and find ways to turn such conflict into a healthy, creative tension. They need to identify where operating styles are likely to clash, and they may have to launch internal education and communications initiatives in order to minimize the harmful effects of conflict and to help staff members agree on appropriate operating styles.

Of course, nonprofit leaders could opt to segregate commercial activities from philanthropic operations. Such an approach should reduce conflict, provided that the separate units do not need to interact on a day-to-day basis. Even so, staff on the more philanthropic side of operations may view their commercial colleagues with animosity or envy. Compensation is one possible source of friction between the two cultures. New hires from the business world may require higher compensation than internal staff members with comparable levels of education and years of experience. Pay equity has to be dealt with explicitly, or it will fester.

A former Wall Street banker who now heads a major international economic-development organization is grappling with precisely this issue. His operations have become increasingly sophisticated and require skills typically held by MBA graduates who could land investment-banking jobs. But he cannot pay anything approaching the investment-banking salaries to acquire the talent he needs. It was a challenge to get his board to let him make offers at salaries less than half those that qualified candidates could command in mainstream financial institutions. Yet even those salaries were well above existing wages in the organization, and the leader was concerned about pay equity with the organization's current staff. Raising everyone's salary could be extremely costly. Not doing so could undermine morale.

Engineering a new culture is never easy or quick. Building internal expertise has to be a deliberate strategic process. It cannot be accomplished overnight. Managers must create a new culture that blends commercial values with the traditional philanthropic principles that drive the organization. At the same time, they must work with key stakeholders to build understanding of and support for commercial activities, or they may find themselves in the awkward position that the AMA faced in its deal with Sunbeam.

Nonprofit leaders also need to get legal and tax advice before launching any commercial activities. Unfortunately, tax laws often lag behind industry developments. It is not always clear how current Internal Revenue Service regulations will treat new hybrid forms of organizations. In some cases, it will be better to set up a for-profit subsidiary and pay the appropriate taxes. As the boundaries between nonprofit and for-profit organizations fade, pressure will mount for new regulations and possible revisions in the tax code. Becoming more commercial has political risks and puts the burden of proof on social entrepreneurs to show that their organizations are serving social missions that justify continued tax exemption.

Steering into New Seas

Thoughtful innovation in the social sector is essential if organizations are to leverage limited philanthropic resources. Nonprofit leaders can benefit from finding effective ways to harness commercial forces for social good. But misguided efforts to reinvent nonprofits in the image of business can go wrong. Nonprofit managers are only beginning to learn what it means to search for new solutions to social problems and for more effective ways to deliver socially important goods.

Strategic and structural innovation should focus on improving mission-related performance. Caught up in the current wave of commercialization, nonprofits risk forgetting that the most important measure of success is the achievement of mission-related objectives, not the financial wealth or stability of the organization. The benefit of finding attractive sources of earned income lies more in the leverage this income provides than its sustainability. But generating more funds for ineffective or inefficient programs is not a productive use of resources. True social-sector entrepreneurs are those who find not only additional sources of funds but also new methods to link funding to performance. More important, they develop more effective ways to improve conditions on this planet. To that end, social entrepreneurs shouldn't focus on commercial approaches alone but should explore all strategic options along the social enterprise spectrum, including their ability to use social causes to tap into philanthropic motivations. In fact, multi-unit operations may well be the wave of the future because they recognize and, when it makes sense, utilize a full range of options on the social enterprise spectrum.

In the end, for-profit operations will not—and should not—drive out philanthropic initiatives.

In the end, commercial operations will not—and should not—drive out philanthropic initiatives. Many worthwhile objectives cannot effectively be pursued by relying on market mechanisms alone. In any case, people tend to get something out of giving that they cannot get out of market transactions. People want to make contributions to the common good, or to their vision of it. The challenge is to harness these social impulses and marry them to the best aspects of business practice in order to create a social sector that is as effective as it can be.

Related Readings

Jed Emerson And Fay Twersky, co-editors. *New Social Entrepreneurs: The Success, Challenge, and Lessons of Nonprofit Enterprise Creation.* San Francisco, CA: Roberts Foundation, 1996.

Ronald Grzywinski. "The New Old-Fashioned Banking." HBR May–June 1991.

David C. Hammack and Dennis R. Young, editors. *Nonprofit Organizations in a Market Economy: Understanding New Roles, Issues, and Trends.* San Francisco, CA: Jossey-Bass Publishers, 1993.

Alice Howard and Joan Magretta. "Surviving Success: An Interview with the Nature Conservancy's John Sawhill." HBR September–October 1995.

William H. Shore. *Revolution of the Heart: A New Strategy for Creating Wealth and Meaningful Change.* New York, NY: Riverhead Books, 1995.

Edward Skloot, editor. *The Nonprofit Entrepreneur:*

Creating Ventures to Earn Income. New York: The Foundation Center, 1988.

Richard Steckel with Robin Simons and Peter Lengsfelder. *Filthy Rich and Other Nonprofit Fantasies: Changing the Way Nonprofits Do Business in the 90s.* Berkeley, CA: Ten Speed Press, 1989

Originally published in January–Febraury 1998
Reprint 98105

The author would like to thank Elaine Backman for her contributions to the development of the social enterprise spectrum.

Do Better at Doing Good

V. KASTURI RANGAN,

SOHEL KARIM, AND

SHERYL K. SANDBERG

Executive Summary

IN SPITE OF TOP-NOTCH EFFORTS, many social-
change initiatives fail. What goes wrong? How can the
initiatives be presented more effectively? Analyzing the
costs and benefits of the proposed change from the perspective of the targeted community can help marketers
answer those questions. The authors present a framework to facilitate such an analysis and to help form
effective marketing plans.

When the proposed behavior change involves little
cost to the targeted community and provides a significant personal benefit, conventional marketing methods—
such as those used for marketing consumer goods—can
be effective. The task becomes more challenging when
the targeted community cannot perceive an immediate
personal benefit and thus lacks the motivation to change
its behavior. In such cases, it may be possible to

overcome the inertia by making the proposed change as easy as possible to implement.

When the proposed change involves a high cost, in terms of either money or some other measure (difficulty, for instance, in quitting smoking), the social marketer's job becomes harder. The campaign must not only communicate effectively, it must also provide any support that the targeted community will need in order to comply.

Social marketers face their greatest challenge in cases where the cost is high and the personal benefit is intangible. In some instances, it may be possible for the marketers to change the focus of the campaign; another approach is to persuade a small portion of the targeted community to change their behavior and then to leverage the power of those early adopters. Moral persuasion and peer pressure can help over the long term as well.

IN THE MID-1980S, several major antidrug initiatives, targeted at school-age children, were launched in Boston. A significant amount of media time and space was devoted to public-service announcements designed by top-notch advertising talents. The ads were brief, clear, and informative. In 1987, however, market surveys revealed that although many people remembered the campaigns, the effort at social change had been, in large part, unsuccessful. The initiatives did not persuade their target audience to change its

Unfortunately, conventional marketing methods are not always effective when used in social-change.

behavior. What went wrong? Should the managers spearheading the various campaigns have known better? Could they have planned more effective strategies from the outset?

Quite often, managers in charge of developing marketing strategies for social-change efforts—such as antidrug campaigns, community development programs, or recycling initiatives—rely on conventional, consumer-goods-oriented marketing methods to promote their missions. Unfortunately, such methods are not always effective. Conventional marketing methods are generally designed for situations in which benefits to the consumer from choosing the advertised product or service clearly outweigh

Many social-marketing programs are bedeviled by a what's-in-it-for-me reaction from their targets.

the costs. Choosing a particular credit-card company because it offers a low interest rate is a clear-cut proposition with a tangible reward. So is purchasing an automobile with a certain set of features. With social marketing, however, the benefits are not always so concrete. They often accrue to society, sometimes over the long term. In fact, in some cases, the individuals, communities, or organizations targeted by the change effort may feel that the costs of change exceed the benefits.

For example, most people in the developed world are well aware of the harmful consequences of deforestation. Yet one would hardly expect a logging laborer in Brazil to stop cutting trees, even if the long-term consequences of his actions were made clear to him. If he changed his behavior, he would no longer be able to support his family.

Clearly, not all social-marketing programs are bedeviled by a what's-in-it-for-me reaction from their intended targets. But many are, and such attitudes must be dealt with. We have developed a framework to help social marketers determine which causes can be promoted through conventional marketing methods, which need an alternative approach, and what the options are in the latter case.

Obstacles to Marketing Social Change

Before introducing our framework for assessing social-marketing challenges and planning effective campaigns, we must consider the obstacles facing social marketers in greater detail.

To begin with, in many social-marketing situations, *the target community opposes the change being advocated.* Social change often involves altering people's core attitudes and beliefs as a prelude to changing their behavior. Consider the issue of family planning in Bangladesh. In the late 1970s, government officials determined that the small country, which is the size of the state of Wisconsin, would soon outgrow its limited economic resources if it did not control its population growth rate. With the help of foreign aid, the government launched a massive campaign to curb population growth. Contraceptives for men were given out free at clinics and social workers urged men to practice family planning.

The effort fell short. Why? Because most of the country's citizens did not understand the long-term benefits to the country; they saw only the conflicts between the proposed behavior changes and their way of life, and the problems that such change would bring upon them as individuals. Most parents counted on children to be a support in their old age, because Bangladesh, like many developing nations, does not have a system of pensions or social security for all its citizens. Since many Bangladeshi children die before they reach adulthood—the result of natural calamities such as typhoons and epidemics such as cholera—couples usually had a few "extra" children as a safety margin. Also, in the Bangladeshi social system, tradition dictates that the parents of the bride present the parents of the groom with a cash gift at the wedding, so it made sense to try to have at least as many male children as female to balance the cash flow. Furthermore, a large family would provide sufficient hands for cultivating rice and catching fish, avoiding the necessity of hiring labor outside the family. Finally, there were those among the country's predominantly Muslim population who viewed family planning as an unnatural act that violated their religious faith. It is no wonder the initial campaign was unsuccessful.

Another common obstacle to social change is that, for the target community, *the adoption costs often exceed tangible benefits.* That is certainly the case for the logger—or the logging company—in Brazil being asked to give up work (or profits) to save the rain forest. The same holds true for chemical companies that are asked to stop producing chlorofluorocarbons (CFCs) to protect the earth's fragile ozone layer.

CFCs have been unequivocally identified as destructive of the ozone layer. If CFC production were stopped immediately, it is estimated that by the year 2075 some 3 million lives in the United States alone would be saved from death from skin cancer. Globally, the number would exceed 10 million lives saved. But for the chemical companies that produce CFCs, the cost of terminating production, researching and developing alternatives, and bringing those alternatives to market are an immediate, tangible concern. In 1989, those costs were estimated to be approximately $500 million for each of the dozen or so companies that would be affected. For chemical companies whose main business is producing CFCs, it is difficult to appreciate long-term, societal benefits in the face of the immediate cost, especially since it would be difficult for a third party—a government or foundation, for instance—to provide monetary compensation for ceasing CFC production.

With some social-marketing initiatives, a critical obstacle to implementation is that *early adopters stand to lose*. Again, consider the chemical companies. If only a few companies changed their behavior, those companies would be at a disadvantage in a marketplace where other organizations continued to make and market cheaper, yet environmentally dangerous, products.

Similarly, if only a few couples in Bangladesh chose to have smaller families, those couples would be at a disadvantage among their peers, and there would be no ensuing benefit to society. Schools would become less crowded, food more plentiful, and medical facilities widely available only if the society as a whole reduced its birthrate.

That obstacle brings to light another, related challenge. In conventional marketing situations, if some consumers balk at a new feature or service package, marketers have the option of segmenting the market—identifying and targeting those people for whom their product or service will be attractive. With social-marketing efforts, such flexibility is not always possible. In fact, with many social-change initiatives, *the benefit accrues only when a large percentage of the target community accepts the proposed change.* For example, even if a few chemical companies were more inclined than others to change their behavior, social marketers cannot limit their campaigns to persuading those few to change. The ozone layer's rate of depletion will not decrease measurably until all the major producers of CFCs are on board.

Analyzing the Costs and Benefits of Change

We have developed a framework that allows social marketers to examine the change they are advocating from the potential adopter's perspective and to plan their marketing strategy accordingly. There are four cells located along a vertical axis that represents the cost dimension and a horizontal axis that represents the benefits. (See the chart "The Type of Initiative. . .")

By costs, we mean not only the monetary costs of adopting a behavior but also the costs in terms of time, effort, and any other psychological (or organizational) discomfort the adoption behavior may cause. For example, the cost of smoking cessation is high because giving up cigarettes is tremendously difficult.

Similarly, the benefit dimension includes all nonmonetary advantages that individuals or organizations may gain if they adopt the recommended behavior. These advantages range from physiological benefits and psychological benefits at the individual level to improved corporate image for organizations and environmental or sociological benefits at a societal level.

A principal function of the benefit dimension is to identify the primary beneficiary of any given program for social change. A campaign designed to encourage men to be tested for colon cancer, for example, clearly benefits individuals; an AIDS prevention program, on the other hand, benefits not only the individuals toward whom the campaign is directed but also all potential partners of those individuals. With a recycling initiative, the primary beneficiary is the community or society as a whole. Of course, individuals gain if their community as a whole is better off, but the gain is felt primarily at a societal level and only secondarily at the individual level.

In many cases, the distinctions between beneficiaries are difficult to make; indeed, the lines between individual and societal benefits often overlap. Preventing

Marketers must make clear the benefits of the proposed behavior change to the target community.

and societal benefits often overlap. Preventing or stopping drug abuse benefits individuals, but the change in behavior also fosters a healthier society. For marketing purposes, it is important to try to define the primary beneficiaries as specifically as possble.

The Type of Initiative. . .

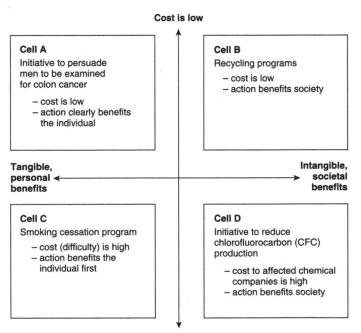

Cost is low

Cell A
Initiative to persuade men to be examined for colon cancer

– cost is low
– action clearly benefits the individual

Cell B
Recycling programs

– cost is low
– action benefits society

Tangible, personal benefits ← → **Intangible, societal benefits**

Cell C
Smoking cessation program

– cost (difficulty) is high
– action benefits the individual first

Cell D
Initiative to reduce chlorofluorocarbon (CFC) production

– cost to affected chemical companies is high
– action benefits society

Cost is high

Determining Appropriate Strategies

Once a manager has determined in which cell the initiative most appropriately belongs, the next step is to consider what kind of marketing plan will be most persuasive for that particular kind of initiative. Each cell presents different marketing problems. (See the chart ". . .and the Challenge It Presents.") Let us consider each of the cells in the framework individually.

CELL A

Here, the cost to the intended beneficiary of changing behavior is relatively small compared to the potential

---

. . . and the Challenges It Presents

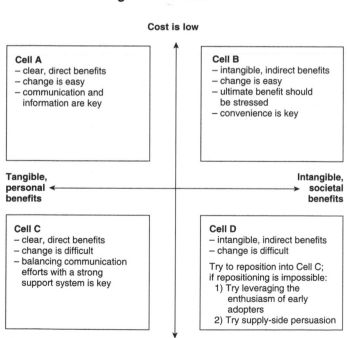

Cost is low

Cell A
– clear, direct benefits
– change is easy
– communication and information are key

Cell B
– intangible, indirect benefits
– change is easy
– ultimate benefit should be stressed
– convenience is key

Tangible, personal benefits ← → **Intangible, societal benefits**

Cell C
– clear, direct benefits
– change is difficult
– balancing communication efforts with a strong support system is key

Cell D
– intangible, indirect benefits
– change is difficult

Try to reposition into Cell C; if repositioning is impossible:
1) Try leveraging the enthusiasm of early adopters
2) Try supply-side persuasion

Cost is high

benefits. The task for marketers is thus similar to persuading consumers to buy conventional products and services. First, the marketer will need to concentrate on communicating the benefits of the proposed behavior change to the target community. Second, the marketer should make sure that any tools or services necessary for adopting the change are readily available.

Consider an initiative designed to persuade middle-aged men to visit their doctors for a colon cancer check. The campaign was created by the Advertising Council, a nonprofit agency based in New York that develops and places close to a billion dollars' worth of public-service announcements every year. Ad Council marketers knew that for a vast majority of males, adopting the behavior change would involve only the minor inconvenience of scheduling and keeping a doctor's appointment. After the examination, most of them would be declared cancer-free. For the unlucky few who would be diagnosed as having a potential cancer, the benefits of early medical attention and treatment would far outweigh the initial costs of making and keeping an appointment.

So the campaign took a conventional approach: It relied on communication to demonstrate the clear value of the change to the targeted individuals. The campaign's most important component was information dissemination. Success depended on the effectiveness of the communication and its reach. The target community—the "customers"—needed to know why it was important to get an early checkup. The campaign sought to create an urgency in the minds of the target population in order to stimulate them to arrange for examinations. Because most doctors and health professionals are well trained in the detection procedure, service availability was not a problem.

It is important to underscore that Cell A campaigns do not need to address deep-rooted beliefs or attitudes. The targets of Cell A campaigns often are merely complacent; they pass up the desired behavior not because they are opposed to it but because they do not have the information that would prompt them to change. But when information is presented, knowledge can quickly lead to persuasion.

Another note on Cell A endeavors: Many social-marketing campaigns unnecessarily oversell the morbid consequences of not adopting the recommended behavior. Some of them employ a heavy-handed tone in an attempt to change underlying attitudes, when simply providing information and support would be more effective. Instead of giving parents information on where and how to get their children immunized, for example, a campaign may get drawn into portraying the disastrous consequence of not adopting the behavior—a child's death. Infrequently, a "fear appeal" may be necessary to shock and goad people to action, but most money and time spent on such approaches are wasted resources—lost opportunities to persuade the audience more reasonably.

CELL B

As with Cell A projects, Cell B projects do not require fundamental shifts in the attitudes or lifestyles of the target population. The problem with Cell B projects is that they may not seem compelling; there are no direct, individual benefits. Marketers facing Cell B challenges need to focus their efforts on providing a catalyst for change in the form of a convenient way for the target population to comply.

Consider the problem of resource conservation at the household level. In the early 1990s, a survey conducted by the Environmental Federation of America (Earth Share) revealed that 74% of respondents supported stronger environmental standards, regardless of cost. This was a considerable jump from a similar survey conducted in the mid-1980s that had shown about 45% support for environmental initiatives. Yet market research company Roper Starch reported in 1992 that fewer than one in ten Americans made personal efforts on a regular basis to help solve environmental problems.

In 1992, fewer than one in ten Americans made personal efforts on a regular basis to help solve environmental problems— even though most supported stronger environmental standards.

Earth Share, hoping to increase participation in resource conservation practices in homes nationwide, retained the Ad Council to develop a communications program supporting environmentally friendly behavior at the household level. The Ad Council's campaign team, in turn, commissioned its own survey of nearly 1,000 men and women to ascertain opinions of 20 environmentally friendly behaviors such as shutting off water while brushing teeth and using energy-efficient lightbulbs. The questions were designed to reveal how important, difficult, and demanding those behaviors seemed, how frequently respondents currently practiced them, and how willing they would be to start practicing the behaviors if they were not doing so currently.

The survey found that respondents were highly sensitive, in general, to environmental issues. Most of the behaviors covered by the survey were rated as highly important. Some of the behaviors (such as using cloth shopping bags or putting a bottle or brick in the toilet tank) were also perceived as easy to adopt. Surprisingly, however, respondents reported that they only rarely practiced these behaviors.

Based on the survey results, the Ad Council determined that the catalyst people needed to change their behavior was simply clear instruction about easy things they could do at home to protect the environment and frequent reminders to do them. So marketers launched a relentless communication campaign reminding the public to adopt the behaviors and showing them how to do so. Over the last few years, as the campaign has matured, the focus of the ads, brochures, and other methods of communication has become increasingly practical. The result has been a sharp increase in household-level conservation practices.

For the purposes of contrast, consider a Cell B challenge with very different parameters: one philanthropist's efforts to promote the development of rural areas in Thailand. With an average annual GNP growth rate of 10% or higher through the late 1980s and early 1990s, Thailand is one of the world's fastest-growing economies. Unfortunately, the disparity between personal incomes in the urban and rural sectors is growing at an even faster rate. The average annual per capita income in the Greater Bangkok area is about $3,000; in Thailand's other provinces, per capita income ranges from $300 to $1,000. In 1989, to address the imbalance, Mechai Viravaidya, a philanthropist known for his work on family planning issues, launched TBIRD: the Thai Business Initiative in Rural Development.

TBIRD had a simple plan. Large private companies doing business in Thailand would each be asked to "adopt" a village in the rural interior and assist in its development. Businesspeople would devote a given amount of time and resources to help villagers boost agricultural productivity and acquire skills in nonagricultural activities. As Mechai said shortly before TBIRD's launch, "If only business could be convinced to voluntarily devote a small portion of their time and resources to address a national development need, we would not need the assistance of bureaucrats and politicians."

But the idea did not take hold very easily. In the overall scheme of things, adopting a village would not be a financial drain on the resources of the large private companies that TBIRD was targeting, but direct benefits to those companies were hard to identify. Many senior managers thought of the initiative as a way to give an indirect gift or a donation rather than as a serious program that would benefit both the rural communities and Thailand as a whole. As a result, TBIRD's first efforts were largely unsuccessful: In its first year of existence, it persuaded fewer than half a dozen companies to join the program.

In order to convince companies that the initiative would be worth their time and money, Mechai had to make the adoption—the process of working with the villagers—convenient and painless. Then he had to rethink the benefits of the effort and create some direct reward for the sponsoring companies. To accomplish those tasks, Mechai and his team developed a process that, among other things, took the following steps: First, TBIRD provided a personal adviser to each company that agreed to participate. Before the company got involved with the village, the adviser would provide a comprehensive assessment of the village's needs. As the program took shape, the adviser would act as a facilitator or mediator between the company and the village leaders. Second, TBIRD advisers would become residents of the designated village or villages until the program was well underway; they would help the company and the village select appropriate projects that would benefit both parties. For example, Bangkok Glass Industry Company, with the help of such an adviser, trained villagers to make brushes for cleaning its glass molds. The company set up a production facility to produce 150 brushes a day. Previously, Bangkok Glass had outsourced such work to other established companies; now it was paying villagers instead. Similarly, in a different village, Singer (Thailand) established a training school to teach young women to sew and followed up with a contract for 600 uniforms.

Slowly, TBIRD repositioned its campaign so that corporate sponsors were drawing direct benefits from their efforts. Equally important, TBIRD's new process made it easier for corporations to adopt the new behavior. The end result? Within two years of the program's reconfiguration, nearly 100 companies were in TBIRD's adoption pipeline.

For this social-marketing challenge, a highly moralistic campaign aimed at creating a sense of guilt in the target community—the area's companies—would have been a complete waste. Indeed, many social-marketing programs in Cell B fail because they take an overly moralistic tone and attempt to evangelize. The key to a Cell B challenge is information *backed up with convenience mechanisms.* A small proportion of a target audience may alter its behavior because of its convictions, but if a behavior change is made easy and if the campaign is persistent enough, even those who were unconvinced may switch.

CELL C

In Cell C, the individual benefits of a behavior change are clear, but the cost of such change is daunting. Social-change campaigns that fall into Cell C thus require a good deal of *push marketing* in addition to strong communication campaigns. In conventional marketing situations, push marketing can be thought of as what happens once a consumer has developed some broad general interest in a product or a service but has not yet decided on purchasing a specific brand. Before making a decision, the consumer may talk with friends or salespeople. He or she may read literature on the product, such as independent reviews or manufacturers' brochures. The consumer is also likely to be exposed to additional promotional material at the point of purchase.

In social-change efforts, push marketing consists of intensive support provided to the target community *at the community level.* Without that support, a Cell C campaign will not succeed. Unfortunately, although many social marketers realize the need for such support, Cell C initiatives are rarely balanced correctly. Many Cell C programs are hopelessly one-sided—they focus either on communication or on intensive support, not on a combination of both.

Consider the unsuccessful antidrug campaign mentioned in the introduction. Initially, it was weighted heavily on the side of communication through advertisements. One advertisement, typical of the sort the campaign used, featured teenage actress Nancy McKeon, who directly addressed viewers with an admonition that drug abuse is dangerous. The message was "Be cool like me. Don't do drugs."

Another ad that received a lot of airtime featured a slow-motion study of an adolescent girl. She is shown first taking drugs with her friends, then being wheeled on a gurney into a hospital emergency room. The soundtrack is the song "Take Me Out to the Ball Game," with the words changed as follows: "Take me out of the ball game;/ Take me out of the crowd;/ Buy me some pieces of crack, Jack;/ I don't care if I never come back . . . ." That ad ended with then-Mayor Raymond Flynn urging Boston's schoolchildren to reject drugs. A final example of the genre showed a teenage boy in his bedroom, obviously strung out on drugs. He addresses the viewer, saying that his parents are "dumb" and that they don't understand him and his need for help. At the ad's conclusion, a voice announces a toll-free hot line to use if a friend or child needs help for a drug problem.

The ads did have some effect: When Flynn commissioned a marketing research team to study the campaign's effects and offer advice on how to proceed, focus groups revealed that the city's school-age children had very high recognition of the antidrug public-service announcements. They could even recall several visual and written elements of the campaigns that had been aired frequently by local television stations, though they found the celebrity messages artificial. The children understood intellectually the harmful effects of drug abuse. Unfortunately, however, they felt unable to change any abusive behavior. The campaign had little or no influence on whether and how often the children took drugs.

The research revealed that many children took drugs because they wanted to be accepted by their peers. Saying no violated their social norms and network. To say no, they needed coping mechanisms. For example, they needed help inventing excuses not to take drugs, because they didn't want to say no outright. They also needed to know where to go to talk about drugs. The research found that parents and teachers were not a preferred outlet; the children felt more comfortable talking with counselors in community centers. In short, the research team concluded that an effective antidrug campaign would have to include not only information but also a strong support system for altered behavior.

Marketers with Cell C problems must go well beyond identifying their target community's behavior and communicating why change is desirable. In order for a Cell C campaign to have an effect, it must also address the context of the challenge. What external factors are influencing the target audience? Will the marketing campaign need to address those as well? If so, how much effort needs to be devoted to support mechanisms? What kinds of follow-up procedures are needed? With the Boston schoolchildren, only a concerted community-support program could insulate the children in the short run while educating them about the harmful consequences of drug abuse and giving them the strength to say no on their own.

CELL D

Displayed here are all the anomalies that make marketing social change so difficult. From the potential adopter's perspective, the cost-benefit ratio in a Cell D endeavor is terribly disadvantageous. The benefits are intangible in the short run and the cost of change is high.

The first thing marketers should do when they have a Cell D challenge on their hands is determine whether the initiative can be repositioned into Cell C. That is, they should try to figure out whether there is some way to show the target community a more direct benefit. Consider the Bangladesh family-planning example. After extensive research, Population Services International (PSI), a nonprofit organization based in Washington, D.C., concluded that although Bangladeshi men were unable to see the long-term economic benefits or quality-of-life considerations associated with family planning, women could. Women indicated that they were receptive to the concept of family planning as a way to improve their health and the health of their existing children. Women also saw that such planning would lead to opportunities for a better education, and, in general, a more prosperous existence. They did not have the same reservations about family planning that men had.

In theory, because the women could see a direct benefit from family planning, the campaign should have been easy to shift into Cell C. The marketers didn't have to design or build in new benefits. The target community as a whole could be persuaded to participate through the commitment of the women. But in practice, such a shift was difficult to accomplish. The marketers had to overcome a strong cultural barrier. In Bangladesh, the men usually did most of the household shopping. They did not generally discuss personal issues such as family size with their wives. And, in any case, women would be embarrassed to buy contraceptives in a public place. PSI's male contraceptives were being widely distributed, but for the family planning program to be truly effective, women had to become empowered consumers.

In order to reposition the program to Cell C, PSI launched a two-pronged effort. First, it made female contraceptives available through the country's 100,000 rural medical practitioners. RMPs participate in village community activities and are respected and regarded as friends, philosophers, and guides by many village people. And since RMPs make house calls, women would be spared the embarrassment of going out to buy contraceptives.

Second, and just as important, PSI mounted a new communication program directed at the men. The aim of that program was to break down cultural barriers and encourage men to discuss family planning issues with their wives. The program—which consisted, in part, of film ads shown at traveling cinema shows—did not seek to cause a cultural revolution by showing females in dominant, decision-making roles. Rather, it co-opted the men by portraying one of their peers discussing the subject with his wife and drawing the conclusion that he should be supportive of the idea.

Today, Bangladesh's family planning program is widely considered a success. In the 1980s, only 4% of targeted Bangladeshi couples practiced family planning. According to the Demographic and Health Survey of Bangladesh, that number has risen in the 1990s to 45%. Other informed sources estimate the number at 60%.

Of course, it is not always possible to move a Cell D project to another cell. If such a shift cannot be accomplished, social marketers first must try to persuade a small portion of the target community to change their behavior and then must leverage the power of those

early adopters. As we have said, early adopters often
stand to lose if the rest of the target group do not
quickly accept and implement the behavior modifica-
tion. But if a few participants become committed to the
cause, it is in their best interest to become active agents
for change. Marketers can use this motivation to great
advantage if they are prepared to guide the early
adopters' enthusiasm.

Think back to the producers of CFCs. The governments of the United States, Canada, Sweden, and Nor-
way banned the use of CFC aerosols in the late 1970s. However, it was not until the mid-1980s, when it was proven that CFCs had indeed dam-aged the ozone layer, that the chemical com-panies themselves began

In the mid-1980s, chemical companies themselves began to work for the elimination of CFC production. With their participation, the effort gained serious momentum.

to act as agents for social change. With their participation, the effort to eliminate CFC production gained serious momentum.

Until the mid-1980s, U.S., European, and Japanese
companies continued to produce CFCs for non-aerosol
applications. Each company knew that acting alone
not only wouldn't solve the problem but also would
put it at a severe disadvantage in the marketplace.
Indeed, even a unilateral U.S. action would have disadvantaged about half a dozen U.S. chemical companies
active in the global market. But with the United States
accounting for nearly 50% of world CFC production
and consumption, the U.S. companies, led by DuPont,
realized that a consortium of chemical companies

could influence the industry. As a result, in 1986, with the active support of U.S. CFC producers, the United States assumed a proactive stance in the United Nations Environmental Program (UNEP), which culminated in the Montreal Protocol of 1987—a landmark agreement that provides for a 50% cut from 1986 levels of CFC production by 1999.

The CFC war is not yet won. But there have been victories, in large part as a result of the ability of international institutions such as the UNEP to provide a forum in which countries can look for a way to protect the ozone layer without concomitant disadvantages for the chemical companies.

Supply-side persuasion—in this case, appealing to the manufacturers of CFCs rather than the consumers—is a viable approach to a Cell D challenge. But other, more indirect approaches can help a cause succeed over the long term as well. Moral persuasion, peer pressure, and demarketing activities aimed at the infrastructure supporting the supplier are effective tactics for both Cell C and Cell D challenges because they influence social and cultural attitudes. Consider the smoking cessation campaigns in the United States. The allure of smoking started to diminish as, one by one, social and cultural mores began to change. Gradually, smoking ceased to be seen as sexy, powerful, liberating, or a sign of success; instead, smokers began to be perceived as people needing help to kick a very bad habit. The burst of scientific evidence—including evidence of the harmful effects of passive smoking—and the response by federal, state, and local governments to

Marketers' enthusiasm can override consideration of the real needs of the intended beneficiaries.

those unequivocal data all served to fuel the antismoking movement. Smoking cessation campaigns, which were once perceived as an attempt to infringe on indi vidual rights, are seen in the 1990s as informative, credible, and useful.

Mission Driven, Market Led

Correctly analyzing the nature of a social-marketing initiative can increase its chances of success, but there are several additional factors to reckon with.

Perhaps the greatest of these is the zeal of the marketers themselves. Many social-change organizations are founded and run by people extremely committed to and enthusiastic about the cause and mission of the organization. Usually they have undertaken personal sacrifices in order to work for a cause that is consistent with their values. But sometimes their enthusiasm overrides consideration of the real needs of the intended beneficiaries of their work. Ask the clients of public-service-advertisement campaign teams that donate their talent and time free to the cause. The clients will tell you that those wonderfully gifted teams often develop ads that convey the teams' vision instead of addressing the clients' needs. Consider the dedication of the voluntary staff in one community center in Boston. Each staff member had his or her own ideas on how to persuade children to stop doing drugs. One pushed sports, another tried to educate children about the life-threatening consequences of drug abuse, and a third counseled the children simply to repudiate drug pushers. Although the research mentioned earlier showed that what the children needed was a way to say no to their peers, none of the counselors could offer them that kind of coping strategy.

190 *Rangan, Karim, and Sandberg*

Our framework urges social marketers to consider the costs and benefits of any given change effort from the viewpoint of the market—the target community. But therein lies another significant tension. Because social-marketing initiatives rely primarily on donors, volunteers, and other funding sources to support their operations, confusion can arise over whether and how much a social-marketing organization should also consider the opinions of its supporters. In order to succeed, social-marketing managers must make the wishes and needs of the various constituencies converge.

That challenge is further complicated by the fact that many social-change organizations lack good systems for measuring performance. Because the goal of the organization is not to enhance profits but to provide an often intangible and complex social good, managers often lack objective data with which to measure the success or failure of their programs.

In the face of such obstacles, social marketers must remain mission driven but market led. It is the only way that they can succeed. Their efforts must be guided first and foremost by a sensitive understanding of the target community. If the needs of the target community are addressed, the message will be more compelling, the means more efficient, and the mission ultimately more successful.

Originally pubished in May–June 1996
Reprint 96308

The authors are grateful to Sanjay Bijawat for his many useful ideas concerning this manuscript.

About the Contributors

ALAN R. ANDREASEN is a professor of marketing at the
School of Business at Georgetown University. He is a specialist in consumer behavior and the application of marketing to
nonprofit organizations, social marketing, and the market
problems of disadvantaged consumers. Professor Andreason
has published more than 100 articles and conference papers
on a variety of topics, including strategic planning, marketing
decision making, consumer behavior, marketing in nonprofit
organizations, consumer satisfaction, marketing regulation,
social marketing, and marketing research. His most recent
books include *Strategic Marketing in Nonprofit Organizations*
(fifth edition), coauthored with Philip Kotler of Northwestern
University; *Cheap But Good Marketing Research*; and *Marketing Social Change*.

WILLIAM G. BOWEN, president of The Andrew W. Mellon
Foundation since 1988, was president of Princeton Univer-
sity from 1972 to 1988. He recently coauthored, with Derek
Bok, *The Shape of the River: Long-Term Consequences of
Considering Race in College and University Admissions*. His
other books include *The Charitable Nonprofits: An Analysis
of Institutional Dynamics and Characteristics*, with Thomas
I. Nygren, Sarah E. Turner, and Elizabeth A. Duffy; *Inside
the Boardroom*; and *In Pursuit of the PhD*, with Neil L.
Rudenstine.

RICHARD P. CHAIT is a professor at the Harvard Graduate School of Education. His research interests focus on the governance of nonprofit organizations, particularly colleges, universities, and independent schools. With Thomas P. Holland and Barbara E. Taylor, he is the author of *Improving the Performance of Governing Boards* and *The Effective Board of Trustees*. Professor Chait chairs the Harvard Seminar for College Trustees and teaches in the Harvard Business School's program on Governing for Nonprofit Excellence.

J. GREGORY DEES is the Miriam and Peter Haas Centennial Professor in Public Service at Stanford University and serves as an entrepreneur-in-residence at the Center for Entrepreneurial Leadership at the Ewing Marion Kauffman Foundation. He has also served as innovator-in-residence at the Mountain Association for Community Economic Development in Berea, Kentucky. Previously, Professor Dees taught at the Harvard Business School as well as at the Yale School of Management and worked as a consultant with McKinsey & Company.

ALLEN GROSSMAN is a senior lecturer of business administration at the Harvard Business School and a visiting scholar at the Harvard Graduate School of Education. He served as president and chief executive officer of Outward Bound USA for six years before stepping down in 1997 to work exclusively on creating high-performance nonprofit organizations and examining the relationship between a nonprofit's management and the social impact of nonprofits. Before joining the nonprofit sector, he was a regional chief executive of Albert Fisher PLC and chairman of the board of Grossman Paper Company, a national distributor of packaging products. During that time, Mr. Grossman served on and chaired a number of nonprofit boards.

REGINA E. HERZLINGER holds the Nancy R. Mcpherson
Professor of Business Administration Chair at Harvard Business School. She is a specialist in nonprofit financial management and control and the health care industry. Her latest
books include *Conducting Your Financial Checkup: A Practical
Guide for Nonprofit Managers and Board Members* and the
bestselling, award-winning *Market-Driven Health Care*, 1998
winner of the Book of the Year Award from the American College of Healthcare Executives. She is also the author of *Financial Accounting and Management Control of Nonprofits*.

THOMAS P. HOLLAND is a professor and director of the
Institute for Nonprofit Organizations at the University of
Georgia and serves as director of the UGA School of Social
Work's Center for Social Services Research and Development.
Over the past 30 years, he has published extensively on the
management and governance of nonprofit organizations. He
is the coauthor of *Improving the Performance of Nonprofit
Boards*, with Dick Chait and Barbara Taylor. Dr. Holland consults nationally with executives and governing boards of nonprofit organizations and teaches graduate courses on nonprofits. He was recently recognized by UGA as Outstanding
Teacher of the Year and by his school as Outstanding Scholar
of the Year.

SOHEL KARIM is vice president and partner at Copernicus, a
consulting firm advising clients on strategic marketing issues.
He consults with companies on both consumer and business-
to-business marketing problems and has worked with clients
in a broad range of industries, including oil, utilities, enter-
tainment, and toys.

CHRISTINE W. LETTS is a lecturer in public policy and
executive director of the Hauser Center for Nonprofit Organizations at Harvard University. She has extensive experience in

private and public management. At the Kennedy School of Government at Harvard, Ms. Letts teaches courses and executive education in nonprofit management, general public management, and organizational change. As the executive director of the Hauser Center, she is responsible for coordinating activities related to building nonprofit curricula and to research and executive education for nonprofit leaders. Her research interests include the organizational performance and impact of funding practices on nonprofit organizations. She is the coauthor, with Allen Grossman and William Ryan, of *Managing Upstream: The Challenge of Creating High Performing Nonprofit Organizations.*

V. KASTURI RANGAN is the Eliot I. Snider and Family Professor of Business Administration at the Harvard Business School. His current research deals with the impact of environmental complexity on interfunctional coordination within the firm, and between the firm and its distribution channels. Professor Rangan's industrial marketing research has appeared in publications such as the *Journal of Marketing,* the *Harvard Business Review,* the *Journal of Retailing, Industrial Marketing Management,* and *Business Horizons.* Professor Rangan has authored four books, including *Going to Market,* which details distribution systems for industrial products, and *Business Marketing Strategy,* which outlines approaches for managing industrial products and markets over their respective life cycles.

WILLIAM RYAN is a consultant based in Cambridge, Massachusetts, who specializes in strategies to strengthen the performance of nonprofit organizations. His research, analysis, and program development help both nonprofits and foundations develop capacity-building strategies that respond to organizational and sector-wide challenges. He is currently investigating the implications of for-profit social service providers, the emergence of alternative nonprofit governance strategies, and the prospects for value-added grant making.

SHERYL K. SANDBERG is the special assistant to the deputy secretary of the U.S. Department of the Treasury. In this capacity, she serves as the chief of staff to the deputy secretary and assists the secretary and deputy secretary in managing of the department and formulating international and domestic policy. Previously, Ms. Sandberg was an associate at McKinsey & Company.

BARBARA E. TAYLOR is the managing director of the Academic Search Consultation Service in Washington, D.C., and previously served as vice president for programs and research at the Association of Governing Boards of Universities and Colleges. She consults with colleges, universities, and other nonprofit organizations in such areas as governing board development, executive search, board-president and board-faculty relations, strategic planning, and institutional conditions assessment. Ms. Taylor is the author or coauthor of seven books, including *Improving the Performance of Governing Boards* and *The Effective Board of Trustees*. She has also published numerous papers, book chapters, and case studies concerning governance, academic strategy, and institutional financial conditions. She is a Trustee of Wittenberg University.

Index

violations of, 1–3, 31–32, 40
push marketing, 182

Red Cross, 145
regulatory compliance com-
    mittee, 49–50
risk
    commercialization and,
        142–146
    corporate alliances and,
        114–115, 120–124
    excessive, 5
    venture capital model and,
        95–96
RMPs. *See* rural medical practi-
    tioners
Roberts, George, 140
Roberts Enterprise Develop-
    ment Fund (Roberts
    Foundation), 140
Robert Wood Johnson Founda-
    tion, 37
Robin Hood Foundation,
    103
Rockefeller, Laurence, 7
Roper Starch Worldwide,
    125–126, 132, 178
rural medical practitioners
    (RMPs), 186

Salvation Army, 31, 48
sanctions, and accountability,
    11–12, 15–16
Scott, Roy, 120
SEC. *See* Securities and
    Exchange Commission
secrecy, 3, 8

Securities and Exchange Com-
    mission (SEC)
    accountability requirements
        and, 8–9
    origin of, 19–21
    sanctions and, 11–12, 15
service offerings by nonprofits
    dissemination of informa-
        tion and, 14
    distribution of expenses
        and, 40–41
    market signals and, 32–33
    public trust and, 31–32
service users, tracking of, 39
Share Our Strength (SOS),
    117–118, 123
Shore, Bill, 129
short-term liquidity measures,
    23
Skloot, Edward, 93–94
small groups, 68
SmithKline Beecham, 120
social change, community
    opposition to, 170–171
social enterprise spectrum,
    135, 147, 154–160
social services
    federal government and,
        92–93, 94, 114, 141
    for-profit, 141–142
SOS. *See* Share Our Strength
staff of nonprofits. *See also*
    CEOs of nonprofits
    commercialization and,
        161–162
    relationship with board
        members, 85–88

risk management and,
95–96
Viravaidya, Mechai, 179–181
volunteers, 13, 84, 189
vouchers, 151
*Warehouses of Wealth: The
Tax-Free Economy* (Gaul
& Borowski), 37
War on Poverty, 94
Washington, D.C. *See* District
of Columbia

Welsh, Jerry, 115
Westinghouse Electric and
Manufacturing Com-
pany, 19
work organization, and boards
of directors, 64–66. *See
also* organizational
capacity

Yale University, 44
YMCA, 142